More REAL STORIES

FOR THE SOUL

More REAL STORIES FOR THE SOUL

THOMAS NELSON PUBLISHERS
Nashville, Tennessee

The Author and Publisher sincerely appreciate all those whose stories are retold or quoted in this book. We have made every effort to quote the source for each story. If we have inadvertently left anyone out, please let us know.

Published in Nashville, Tennessee, by Thomas Nelson, Inc.

Library of Congress Cataloging-in-Publication Data

Morgan, Robert J., 1952–
More real stories for the soul / by Robert J. Morgan
p. cm.
ISBN 0-7852-4517-0
1. Christian biography. I. Title.
BR1700.2 .M657 2000 00–041139
CIP

Printed in the United States of America
1 2 3 4 5 6 — 05 04 03 02 01 00

Preface

I began realizing some of the benefits of storytelling when, in the fifth or sixth grade, I was invited to another classroom to entertain pupils with my tales. The benefit was obvious and immediate. I escaped a long, boring afternoon of arithmetic problems and spelling drills.

My stories must not have gone over very well that day, because I wasn't invited back. But nevertheless—I've been telling stories ever since. In the process, I've discovered more and better benefits. Stories, as Christ showed us through His parables, are little laboratories of the mind where we may test, demonstrate, and communicate truth. They teach us lessons, and they help us enlighten others. They provide entertainment that enriches the soul.

My favorite stories are real stories like the ones in

this book, for they illustrate real grace in the lives of real people. I hope you enjoy each of the accounts in this volume and pass them on to your own children, friends, work associates, congregations, Sunday School classes, or the person sitting beside you on the plane.

He who has a good story to tell has the world in his palms.

To My Mother

EDITH MORGAN

whose first prayer is described in the opening story of this volume and whose prayers in recent years have sustained my life and work.

She departed to be with Jesus as I was finishing this manuscript.

More REAL STORIES

FOR THE SOUL

1

Learning to Pray

Edith Morgan of Roan Mountain, Tennessee, was in the third grade when the Great Depression swept over Appalachia, forcing her brother Donnie, seventeen, to leave the mountains for work in Ohio. The checks he sent home every week allowed the family to survive. But it was a cruel separation. Edith dearly loved her big brother, and a long year passed before he was given a week's vacation.

My school desk was in the center of the room, and I couldn't see out the window. One day as class ended, one of the girls by the window told me she had seen my brother Donnie walking up the road. I got so excited I rushed out the door and started running the two miles home. I outran the wagon that normally took us. I was out of breath when I ran through the door, and sure enough, there was Donnie.

She flew into his arms, crying hysterically. To

console her Donnie reached into his pocket and gave her his fountain pen. She had never had a fountain pen before, and very few of the mountain people did have one. It was the kind that, when turned upside down and unscrewed, could be refilled from a bottle of ink. That pen became her pride and joy.

One day I couldn't find my pen. I had no idea where I had misplaced it. I searched every inch of the house, every room, every closet. It was nowhere to be found, and I was agitated. We had been taught to take our problems to the Lord, so I slipped out behind the pile of lumber in the orchard, got down on my knees, and prayed desperately that God would help me find my pen. But I had prayed many times for other things, and was a little doubtful. So I said to God, "Now, Father, answer this prayer. If you won't do anything else, I ask you to do this."

No sooner had I spoken those words than I felt guilty about them. I started to go to the house, but I turned, got back on my knees, and asked God to forgive me for speaking so brashly. Then I asked Him again to help me find my pen.

Getting up, I went immediately to the house, marched straight to the back bedroom, raised the lid of the old trunk that was full of rags and strings from mother's quilt scraps, and plunged my hand into the scraps. There among the strings and scraps I felt my pen. To this day I don't know how it came to be there. I suspect my mother threw it in there because it made such a mess when I tried to refill it. But regardless, God had answered my prayer. There was no doubt about it.

"And that," says Edith Morgan "is how I first learned that Jesus hears our prayers and answers our sincere requests."

2

"I Must Tell Jesus"

Many New Testament promises have corresponding verses in the Old Testament that reinforce their power. When Peter, for example, said, ". . . casting all your care upon Him, for He cares for you" (1 Peter 5:7), he was but restating David's words in Psalm 55:22: "Cast your burden on the Lord and He shall sustain you; He shall never permit the righteous to be moved."

Elisha A. Hoffman loved those verses. He was born May 7, 1839, in Orwigsburg, Pennsylvania. His father was a minister, and Elisha was introduced to Christ at a young age. He attended Philadelphia public schools, studied science, then pursued the classics at Union Seminary of the Evangelical Association. He worked for eleven years with the Association's publishing house in Cleveland, Ohio. Then, following the death of his young wife, he returned to Pennsylvania and devoted thirty-three years to pastoring Benton Harbor Presbyterian Church.

Hoffman's pastime was writing hymns, many of which were inspired by pastoral incidents. One day, for example, while calling on the destitute of Lebanon, Pennsylvania, he met a woman whose depression seemed beyond cure. She opened her heart and poured on him her pent-up sorrows. Wringing her hands, she cried, "What shall I do? Oh, what shall I do?" Hoffman knew what she should do, for he had himself learned the deeper lessons of God's comfort. He said to the woman, "You cannot do better than to take all your sorrows to Jesus. You must tell Jesus."

Suddenly the lady's face lighted up. "Yes!" she cried, "That's it! I must tell Jesus." Her words echoed in Hoffman's ears, and he mulled them over as he returned home. He drew out his pen and started writing,

I must tell Jesus! I must tell Jesus!
I cannot bear my burdens alone;
I must tell Jesus! I must tell Jesus!
Jesus can help me, Jesus alone.

Hoffman lived to be ninety, preaching the Gospel, telling Jesus his burdens, and giving the church such hymns as *What A Wonderful Savior, Down at the Cross, Are You Washed in the Blood?, Leaning on the Everlasting Arms,* and a thousand more.

Do you have a burden too big to bear? Why not close this book and take a few moments to tell Jesus about it. Take your burden to the Lord, then leave it there by faith, casing all your concerns on Him, for He cares for you.

3

Your Maker Is Your Husband

A wonderful friend of mine, Agnes Frazier, once told me that for fifty years she and her husband, Emit, had morning Bible reading and prayer at the breakfast table. On the day he died, she went to bed thinking that she could never again start the day with devotional exercises. But the next morning she bravely sat at the kitchen table and opened her Bible to the spot where she and her husband had quit their reading twenty-four hours before, Isaiah 54. The verse that stared up at her was verse 5: *For your Maker is your husband, The Lord of hosts is His name . . . .*

She smiled and said, "Thank you, Lord."

4

Teamwork

The legendary coach of Alabama's Crimson Tide, Bear Bryant, once said: *I'm just a plowhand from Arkansas, but I have learned how to hold a team together. How to lift some men up, how to calm down others, until finally they've got one heartbeat together, a team. There's just three things I'd ever say: "If anything goes bad, I did it. If anything goes semi-good, then we did it. If anything goes real good, then you did it."*

5

"Smog in My Soul"

One day, as I was caught in bumper-to-bumper traffic, my mind inhaled a dense cloud of "spiritual smog." Feelings of guilt filtered through my heart like toxic fumes, choking it with regret and raw memories. I was en route to an early morning breakfast, and I hadn't slept well. Too much on my mind. Too busy. My defenses were low, and the poisonous vapors seeped in.

I recalled a cruel word that I had written about a woman who was now dead. I saw the face of a man, name forgotten, whom I had struck in a moment's passion. I remembered my failure to witness to a neighbor who later committed suicide. Acts, thoughts, and habits, some only recently confessed to God, came to mind. I felt sick.

Christians are often seized by guilt for sins that are already confessed and forgiven. Like many other believers, I have felt sadness, shame, lingering regret, wafting depression—smog in my soul. It's one thing to confess sin; it's another thing to accept forgiveness.

The Psalmist David said, "My guilt has overwhelmed me like a burden too heavy to bear. My wounds fester and are loathsome because of my sinful folly." David too lived with regret.

But as I gripped my steering wheel, another of David's psalms came to mind—Psalm 103:12: "As far as the east is from the west, so far has He removed our transgressions from us."

The distance between east and west is infinity. The two never meet. Charles Spurgeon wrote, "If sin be removed so far, then we may be sure that the scent, the trace, the very memory of it, must be entirely gone."

I pondered this. When God forgives sin, He forgives it completely—as though it had never occurred.

But when I continue to brood over sin that God has already forgiven, I underestimate His love, doubt His grace, and discount the scope of His pardon. It is as though I fear that the death of Jesus Christ is not adequate, that His blood is too weak to justify me.

Accepting God's forgiveness, on the other hand,

aligns my thinking to God's Word. It separates my sin from my forgiveness by the distance of infinity.

Psalm 103:12 dispersed my noxious thoughts. As my mind cleared, so did the traffic, and I traveled on with joy.* ❧

Decision Magazine, March 1998.

6

The 100-Year-Old Prayer Meeting

In 1722, Count Nicholas Ludwig von Zinzendorf, troubled by the suffering of Christian exiles from Bohemia and Moravia, allowed them to establish a community on his estate in Germany. The center became known as Herrnhut, meaning "Under the Lord's Watch." It grew quickly and so did its appreciation for the power of prayer.

On August 27, 1727, twenty-four men and twenty-four women covenanted to spend an hour each day in scheduled prayer, praying in sequence around the clock. Soon others joined the prayer chain. More signed on, then others still. Days passed, then months. Unceasing prayer rose to God twenty-four hours every day as someone—at least one person—was engaged in intercessory prayer each hour of every day. The intercessors met weekly for encouragement and to read letters and messages from their brothers in different places, giving them specific needs to pray about. A decade passed, the prayer chain continuing nonstop. Then another decade. It was a prayer meeting that lasted over one hundred years.

Undoubtedly this prayer chain helped birth Protestant missions. Six months into it, Zinzendorf, twenty-seven, suggested the possibility of attempting to reach others for Christ in the West Indies, Greenland, Turkey, and Lapland. Twenty-six Moravians stepped forward the next day to volunteer. The first missionaries, Leonard Dober and David Nitschmann, were commissioned during an unforgettable service on August 18, 1732, during which one hundred hymns were sung. The two men reached the West Indies in December of that year, beginning the "Golden Decade" of Moravian Missions, 1732–1742. During the first two years, twenty-two missionaries perished and two more were imprisoned, but others took their places. In all, seventy Moravian missionaries flowed from the six hundred inhabitants of Herrnhut, a feat unparalleled in missionary history.

By the time William Carey became the "Father of Modern Missions," over three hundred Moravian missionaries had already gone to the ends of the earth. And that's not all. The Moravian fervor sparked the conversions of John and Charles Wesley and indirectly ignited the Great Awakening that spread through Europe and America, sweeping thousands into the kingdom. The prayer meeting lasted one hundred years. The results will last for eternity.

7

Unlikely Places

Vance Havner once noted that many college professors are searching for wisdom while the janitors that clean their offices may have discovered it years ago. As an example of that, consider the case of Alexander Grigolia, who immigrated to America from Soviet Georgia early in the twentieth century. He was a brilliant man, and in time he learned English, earned three doctoral degrees, and become a successful professor at the University of Pennsylvania. But despite his freedom and achievements, he had a misery in his heart that he couldn't dislodge. There was an emptiness within he couldn't escape.

One day while getting a shoeshine, he noticed that the bootblack went about his work with a sense of joy, scrubbing and buffing and smiling and talking. Finally

Dr. Grigolia could stand it no longer. He said in his funny-sounding accent, "What always you so happy?"

Looking up, the bootblack paused and replied, "Jesus. He love me. He died so God could forgive my badness. He make me happy."

The professor snapped his newspaper back in front of his face, and the bootblack went back to work.

But Dr. Grigolia never escaped those words, and they brought him eventually to the Savior. He later became a professor of anthropology at Wheaton College, and taught, among others, a young student named Billy Graham.

Augustine wrote in his *Confessions* about his professors: *They saw many true things about the creature (creation) but they do not seek with true piety for the Truth, the Architect of Creation, and hence they do not find Him.*

But some do, and sometimes in the most unlikely places.

8

The Hidden World of Our Thoughts

Meditating on Scripture is vital to a healthy Christian life. Dawson Trotman, founder of the Navigators, frequently lectured his men about the importance of going to sleep while meditating on a verse of Scripture. He knew that our slumbering and subconscious minds tend to mull over whatever we've last inserted into them. When we go to sleep meditating on a Bible verse, it stays with us all night long and we inevitably awaken the next morning in a better frame of mind.

Once as a young pastor I was struggling with a passage of Scripture, trying to find a sermon outline. I had an out-of-town engagement, so I studied in my motel room until the wee hours of the night. That night, I dreamed I was preaching a sermon from that very text, and the outline was clear and easy to follow. Upon waking the next morning, I jotted down the outline I had dreamed up, and I preached that very sermon the next Sunday.

The great British preacher Charles Spurgeon once reportedly preached an entire sermon aloud in his sleep. His wife jotted it down, and he used it in the pulpit the following week. And, in October of 1920, Dr. Frederick Banting was working on his lecture for the following day. His medical practice was too new to be lucrative, so he supplemented his income by teaching. He worked far into the night on the problem of diabetes, but medical science provided scant data on the dreaded disease, and no cure had yet been discovered.

He fell asleep. At two in the morning, he awoke with a start. Grabbing a notebook, he penned three short sentences, then collapsed again in sleep. But those three sentences led to the discovery of insulin.

Still a century earlier, Elias Howe's fertile mind had imagined the sewing machine. He worked and worked on his invention, but its stitches were jagged and uneven, and he grew so frustrated he considered giving up. One night, Howe dreamed that a tribe of savages had kidnapped him. They threatened to kill him if he didn't invent a sewing machine in twenty-four hours. In his dream, he worked frantically but in the end he failed. He was tied for his execution, and the natives raised their spears and flung them in his direction. But as the spears flew at him, Howe noticed they had holes near their tips. He awoke with an idea: put the eye of the needle near the tip.

He patented his sewing machine in 1846.

The words *mull, mill,* and *meal* all come from an Old English word meaning the pulverizing of corn in a grinder. To mull over a subject is to ponder it, to pulverize it in the millstones of the mind. When that subject is Scripture, our souls are fed with manna from heaven.

9

Lottie Moon

Multiplied millions of dollars have poured into overseas missions under the banner of Lottie Moon, the Southern Baptist whose name is used to promote that denomination's annual missionary offering.

But who was Lottie Moon and what did she do?

Lottie (short for Charlotte) was born in 1840 and grew up in an old Virginia family. Her father's plantation house, Viewmont, overlooked the Blue Ridge Mountains. Her mother, a staunch Christian, read to her from the Bible, and as a girl Lottie developed a love for Scripture and for missionary biography. Since there was no church nearby, Mrs. Moon conducted services herself every Sunday for family, neighbors, and servants.

Lottie excelled in school and became one of the first Southern women to earn a Master's Degree, all the while pondering what to do with her life. In the spring of

1873, Lottie, age thirty-three, heard a sermon on John 4:35: *Do you not say, "There are still four months and then comes the harvest?" Behold, I say to you, lift up your eyes and look at the fields, for they are already white for harvest!*

As the preacher spoke of the whitened fields, Lottie made up her mind then and there to become a missionary to China. By autumn she was on her way. When her ship was caught in a terrific storm and appeared to be sinking, she wrote: *As I watched the mad waste of waters, howling as if eager to engulf us, I think I should scarcely have been surprised to see a Divine Form walking upon them, so sweetly I heard in my inmost soul the consoling words, "It is I, be not afraid."*

For forty years, Lottie Moon worked unafraid in North China, serving faithfully amid storms of war, disease, poverty, and plague. When, in her early seventies, a terrible famine swept China, she gave her food and her last dollar for famine relief. She grew so frail and undernourished the doctor ordered her home. She died en route on Christmas Eve, 1912.

"I would that I had a thousand lives that I might give them to the women of China," she said.

She gave her one life, and it has been multiplied a thousandfold.

In a sense, the same is true for us all. As we go about doing good, serving Christ and our world, we're doing more than we know. The Lord multiplies our efforts. As the old song says: "Little is much if God is in it."

Only in heaven will the thousand-fold harvests be seen.

10

John Ploughman

"Whenever a new book comes out," wrote John Ruskin, "I read an old one." Ruskin knew that shallow minds devour books-of-the-moment, but wiser readers digest authors of the past who still speak volumes. With that it mind, I'd like to recommend your spending a quiet evening with John Ploughman.

Ploughman was the creation of British pastor Charles Haddon Spurgeon (1834–1892). Spurgeon is called "The Prince of Preachers," but he could well be dubbed "The King of Classics." He is arguably Christian history's best-selling author with more words in print than anyone else, living or dead. In all, he wrote 135 books and edited another twenty-eight. If we include pamphlets, the total number of Spurgeon's volumes rises to two hundred. His collected sermons stand as the largest set of books by a single author in the history of Christianity.

Not bad for a country boy who never attended college, who suffered debilitating bouts of gout and depression, who cared for an invalid wife, and who died at age fifty-seven.

But Spurgeon enjoyed a phenomenal mind and exceptional gifts. He read six books a week, preached as many as ten times Sunday-to-Sunday, and once said he counted eight sets of thoughts passing through his mind at the same time while preaching. He was seldom heard by fewer than six thousand listeners, and on one occasion his audience numbered nearly twenty-four thousand—all this before the days of microphones and mega-churches.

In 1865, Spurgeon launched a magazine called *The Sword and the Trowel* in which he regularly included maxims under the penname of John Ploughman. The character was actually based on an old farmer, Will Richardson, in Spurgeon's hometown of Stambourne. As a boy, Spurgeon had spent many an hour in the furrows behind Richardson's plow, listening to the man's homespun quips, quotes, comments, and common sense. Years later, in his garden house where *The Sword and the Trowel* was edited, Spurgeon's mind wandered back to those scenes as he composed Ploughman's proverbs.

John Ploughman quickly became for Spurgeon what Poor Richard had been for Benjamin Franklin—his most popular character. When the proverbs were collected and issued as *John Ploughman's Talks,* it became his best-selling book, leading to a sequel, *John Ploughman's Pictures.*

In his *Talks,* John Ploughman covers topics like: Grumblers . . . Debt . . . Things Not Worth Trying . . . Patience . . . Men Who Are Down . . . Very Ignorant People . . . Fault . . . Hope . . . Home . . . and the Preacher's Appearance.

Modern readers will find the language and farming allusions dated, and the ideas Victorian, but the wisdom is enduring. Listen, for example, to Ploughman's thoughts about thinking: *Some will say they cannot help having bad thoughts; that may be, but the question is, do they hate them or not? Vain thoughts will knock at the door, but we must not open to them. Though sinful thoughts rise, they must not reign. He who turns a morsel over and over in his mouth, does so because he likes the flavor, and he who meditates upon evil, loves it, and is ripe to commit it. Snails leave their slime behind them, and so do vain thoughts.*

Good thoughts are blessed guests, and should be heartily welcomed, well fed, and much sought after. Like rose leaves, they give out a sweet smell if laid up in the jar of memory. They cannot be too much cultivated; they are a crop which enriches the soil.

Someone once defined a proverb as a "Heavenly Rule for Earthly Living." It is when the *wit* of one becomes the *wisdom* of many. The ability to distill and condense great truths in simple, quotable statements makes for unique literature, and everyone from King Solomon to Yogi Berra has tried his hand at it.

Spurgeon's fertile mind produced pithy adages and precepts like amber waves of grain, and we can still reap the harvest. Just set aside your modern bestseller awhile, put your hand to the Ploughman, and don't look back.

11

By Prayer Alone

"When I get out to China," a rookie missionary once said to himself, "I shall have no claim on anyone for anything. My only claim will be on God. How important to learn, before leaving England, to move man, through God, by prayer alone."

The rookie was J. Hudson Taylor, who went on to become one of the most famous missionaries in history, opening up the interior of China to the gospel and establishing China Inland Mission (now OMF International). His life's story is a testimony of moving men, women, and even the elements, through God, by prayer alone.

For example, when first sailing for China in 1854, Hudson had been conducting morning worship aboard ship one Sunday when he noticed the captain seemed deeply troubled. Hudson soon learned the reason. A four-knot current was carrying the ship toward some sunken reefs, and there was no wind for navigation. The ship and its passengers were in peril.

"Well, we have done everything that can be done," the captain told Hudson.

"No, there is one thing we have not done yet," replied the missionary.

"What is that?"

"Four of us on board are Christians. Let us each retire to his own cabin, and in agreed prayer ask the Lord to give us immediately a breeze. He can as easily send it now as at sunset."

The captain agreed, and the men did so. Hudson later said he had a "good but very brief session in prayer, and then felt so satisfied that our request was granted that I could not continue asking, and very soon went up again on deck."

The first officer, a godless man, was in charge, and Hudson went over and asked him to let down the corners of the mainsail.

"What would be the good of that?" snapped the man. Hudson told him they had been asking a wind from God and that it was coming immediately. Since they were about to crash into the reef, there wasn't a moment to lose. The man swore and looked at Hudson with contempt. But his eye couldn't help glancing in the direction of the sails. Sure enough, the top corner was beginning to flutter. The crew scrambled to lower the sails, and shortly the vessel was ploughing through the sea at six or seven knots an hour, away from destruction, pushed on its way by winds sent by God.

"Thus God encouraged before landing on China's shores to bring a variety of need to Him in prayer," Hudson recounted, "and to expect that He would honor the name of the Lord Jesus and give the help each emergency required."

Years later, as head of China Inland Mission, Hudson and his colleagues felt impressed to ask God for three things: One hundred new missionaries, an extra $50,000 for their support, and that the money would come in large sums so that the small staff in the home office wouldn't be overwhelmed with record-keeping.

Others, hearing about Hudson's prayer, scoffed. But that year, 102 new missionaries were sent out, $55,000 in extra income came in, and the extra income came as a result of just eleven gifts, scarcely adding to the staff's work.

Then one morning near the end of his life, Hudson was traveling with family and friends through a remote area of China. It was a rigorous journey, and the entire group was exhausted and hungry. They were completely out of food and could find none to buy. While the others started to worry, Hudson began singing, "We thank Thee, Lord, for this our food."

"What food?" asked his companions, "Where is it?"

Hudson replied with a smile, "It cannot be too far away. Our Father knows we are hungry and will send our breakfast soon, but you will have to wait and say your grace when it comes, while I shall be ready to begin eating at once." Within moments they met a man selling cooked rice, and the travelers had a belated but much-appreciated breakfast.

"The prayer of a righteous man," says James 5:16, "is powerful and effective" (NIV).

12

Whipping in Boston Commons

When our children were younger, we read to them every night. Among our favorite books was *Make Way for Ducklings,* Robert McCloskey's classic little book about a mother duck and her chicks who lived in Boston and frequented Boston Commons.

It was a special treat, then, when we visited Boston Commons one summer and rode the famous Swan Boats with our youngsters.

Several years later, I read another story about Boston Commons that told of an incident that once happened there far removed from the joy of ducklings and Swan Boats. It was a brutal flogging and one of America's most deplorable cases of religious persecution.

In 1651, Obadiah Holmes, a Baptist, was arrested

for preaching the gospel in Lynn, Massachusetts, a suburb of Boston. The area was strongly Puritan at the time, and Baptist doctrines were forbidden. When an offer of release was made, pending his paying a fine, Obadiah refused on principle. Friends tried to pay it for him, but he wouldn't let them. His punishment was decreed by authorities. He would be whipped.

On September 6, 1651, he was taken to Boston Commons and commanded to strip to the waist. He was then tied to a whipping post, which became his pulpit. He later wrote: *As the man began to lay the strokes upon my back, I said to the people, Though my flesh should fail, yet God would not fail. So it pleased the Lord to come in and fill my heart and tongue, and with an audible voice I broke forth praying unto the Lord not to lay this sin to their charge.*

In truth, as the strokes fell upon me, I had such a manifestation of God's presence as the like thereof I never had nor felt, nor can with fleshy tongue express, and the outward pain was so removed from me, that indeed I am not able to declare it to you. It was so easy to me that I could well bear it, yea and in a manner felt it not although it was grievous, the man striking with all his strength (spitting on his hands three times as many affirmed) with a three corded whip, giving me therewith thirty strokes. When he loosed me from the post, having joyfulness in my heart and cheerfulness in my countenance, I told the magistrates, "You have struck me with roses."

If so, they were covered with thorns. The whipping was so severe that blood ran down Holmes' body until his shoes overflowed. A friend reported: "Holmes was whipt thirty stripes in such an unmerciful manner that in many days, if not some weeks, he could take no rest, but lay on knees and elbows, not being able to suffer any part of his body to touch the bed."

But the suffering wasn't wasted. The trial and whipping of Obadiah Holmes occasioned the conversion of Henry Dunster, president of Harvard University, to the Baptists, and led to the organization of Boston's first Baptist church.

13

The Privileges of Aging

In October, 1999, in a letter to his "elderly brothers and sisters," Pope John Paul II spoke candidly of his own "twilight years," and of his desire to remain zealous to the end. He wrote, "These are years to be lived with a sense of trusting abandonment into the hands of God, our provident and merciful Father. It is a time to be used creatively for deepening our spiritual life through more fervent prayer and commitment."

"Despite the limitation brought on by age," he continued, "I continue to enjoy life. It is wonderful to be able to give oneself to the very end for the sake of the Kingdom of God. At the same time, I find great peace in thinking of the time when the Lord will call me: from life to life!"

Also meditating on her age, Pearl Buck wrote at age eighty: *I have reached an honorable position in life because I am old and no longer young. I am a far more useful person than I was fifty years ago, or forty years ago, or thirty, twenty, or even ten. I have learned so much since I was seventy.*

Mischa Elman was a Russian-born violinist whose career spanned his entire life. He began performing when unusually young and continued into old age. Someone once asked him if he could tell any difference in audience reaction through the encircling years. "Not really," he replied. "When I was a boy, audiences would exclaim, 'Imagine playing the violin like that at his age!' Now, they're beginning to say the same thing again!"

"It's attitude, not arteries, that determines the vitality of our maturing year," said J. Oswald Sanders. ❧

14

Two Eyes and a Leg

Recently I found an old book in a London shop, *Memories of the Mission Field* by Christine I. Tinling, undated, published in England. It tells of a Swedish missionary, Mr. Tornvall, who arrived in Ping-Liang, China, uninvited and unwelcome. The missionary realized he would only be accepted by providing medical help, but he had no training—*only one small book and some homeopathic remedies.*

He began with an old woman, nearly blind, who was carried each day to ask alms. At night she was returned to her hut where a large stone was rolled across the door to keep out wolves, and there she had to stay until friends removed the stone the next morning. Tornvall stopped daily and treated her eyes with a salve. To the surprise of all, her eyesight was restored.

A soldier was then brought to Tornvall with a frostbitten leg requiring amputation. *I had no instruments except a Swedish penknife and an American saw, but I boiled them and did the best I could. I had a book on anatomy, and I kept it by me during the operation and looked at the diagrams to the leg as I cut. I did it on the verandah, and the neighbors gathered round to watch the performance. I had no ether or chloroform, but used a hot salt solution as a palliative.*

The operation was successful, and afterward the young soldier dried his dismembered leg in the sun so he could carry it home to his mother.

But the city fathers, unimpressed, called a public meeting to discuss driving Tornvall from their boundaries. The tide turned when the old beggar woman faced the crowd. "Do you want good people in this city or not?" she demanded. "You all know me, you know that I was almost blind, and now I see. This man has helped me."

Her words, strangely similar to those in John 9, moved the city, and Tornvall was allowed to stay in Ping-Liang where in time he established both a church and a medical center.

It's often said, "God is not as interested in ability as in availability." He can do amazing things with one small book and homeopathic remedies in the hands of a committed soul.

15

John Craig

John Craig was born in Scotland in 1512, studied at the University of St. Andrews, and entered the ministry. While living on the continent, he found a copy of Calvin's *Institutes* and in reading them found himself becoming a Protestant. As a result, he was arrested by agents of the Inquisition, taken prisoner to Rome, and condemned to death at the stake. On the evening of August 19, 1559, while awaiting execution the next day, dramatic news arrived that Pope Paul IV had died. According to custom, the prisons in Rome were thrown open, and the prisoners were temporarily released.

Craig took advantage of the opportunity, escaping to an inn on the city's outskirts. A band of soldiers tracked him down, but as the captain of the guard arrested him, he paused, looking at him intently. Finally he asked Craig if he remembered helping a wounded soldier some years before in Bologna. "I am the man you relieved," said the captain, "and providence has now put it into my power to return the kindness—you are at liberty." The soldier gave Craig the money in his pockets and marked out an escape route for him.

As he made his way through Italy, Craig avoided public roads, taking the circuitous route suggested by the captain and using the money for food. But at length Craig's money was exhausted, and so were his spirits. He lay down in the woods and gloomily considered his plight. Suddenly the sound of steps was heard, and Craig tensed. It was a dog, and in its mouth, a purse. Craig waved the animal away, fearing a trick. But the dog persisted, fawned on him, and left the purse in his lap.

Using money from the purse, Craig reached Austria where Emperor Maximilian listened to his sermon and gave him safe conduct. He thus returned to his native Scotland where he preached Christ and abetted the Reformation until his death many years later at age eighty-eight.

16

Just As I Am

She was an embittered woman, Charlotte Elliott of Brighton, England. Her health was broken, and her disability had hardened her. "If God loved me," she muttered, "He would not have treated me this way."

Hoping to help her, a Swiss minister named Dr. Cesar Malan visited the Elliotts on May 9, 1822. Over dinner, Charlotte lost her temper and railed against God and family in a violent outburst. Her embarrassed family left the room, and Dr. Malan, left alone with her, stared at her across the table.

"You are tired of yourself, aren't you?" he said at length. "You are holding to your hate and anger because you have nothing else in the world to cling to. Consequently, you have become sour, bitter, and resentful."

"What is your cure?" asked Charlotte.

"The faith you are trying to despise."

As they talked, Charlotte softened. "If I wanted to become a Christian and to share the peace and joy you possess," she finally asked, "what would I do?"

"You would give yourself to God just as you are now, with your fightings and fears, hates and loves, pride and shame."

"I would come to God just as I am? Is that right?"

Charlotte did come just as she was. Her heart was changed that day, as time passed she found and claimed John 6:37 as a special verse for her: ". . . he who comes to Me I will by no means cast out."

Several years later, her brother, Rev. Henry Elliott, was raising funds for a school for the children of poor clergymen. Charlotte wrote a poem, and it was printed and sold across England. The leaflet said: *Sold for the Benefit of St. Margaret's Hall, Brighton: Him That Cometh to Me I Will in No Wise Cast Out.* Underneath was Charlotte's poem—which has since become the most famous invitational hymn in history:

Just as I am, without one plea,
But that Thy blood was shed for me,
And that Thou bidd'st me come to Thee,
O Lamb of God, I come! I come!

Just as I am, and waiting not
To rid my soul of one dark blot,
To Thee whose blood can cleanse each spot,
O Lamb of God, I come! I come!

17

The Hidden Life of Dogs

God must love dogs, because He has made so many of them. And He must have a sense of humor, because He has sometimes used dogs in the oddest ways.

In one of the African churches under the care of missionary James King, there was a lady who came by herself to every service. Accompanying her was an old, ugly dog. He would enter with the lady and sit beside her during the service. She sat on an outside seat next to the aisle, and at the conclusion of the service, when the invitation was given by the pastor for people to come for prayer, the dog would come along and take his place beside her.

The lady's husband was a cruel man, and he abused her. In fact, he beat her so severely that she died. After her death, it was only he and the dog left. But he noticed that the dog disappeared on Wednesday evening about 7:00 and didn't reappear for two hours. It happened again on Sunday morning at about 9:00. The same thing happened Sunday evening.

The following Sunday morning, the man's curiosity was so aroused that he decided to follow and see what the dog was up to. He followed the dog to the humble little church, and the dog went in and took his seat on the aisle while the service went on. At the close of the service, the dog came forward and took his place by the altar.

The man sat in the back of the church, and he was so impressed and touched in his spirit, that he, too, went forward and gave his life to Christ.

And now the dog comes to church with a new master.*

*Adapted from *Parables, Etc.,* January 1987, p. 4.

18

From That Moment

Few missionaries have enjoyed such success as Jonathan and Rosalind Goforth of China. Their ministry swept multitudes into the kingdom and left an army of Christian workers in its wake. Rosalind, however, almost didn't make it to China because of her mother's protests. Writing years after the incident, she recalled a day when her mother vehemently forbade her continued involvement with missionary candidate Jonathan Goforth.

I replied quietly, but firmly, "Mother, it is too late; I promised Jonathan last night to be his wife and go to China!"

Poor Mother! She almost fainted. For six weeks, I stayed with a brother, then came a letter from my sister pleading with me to return, as Mother was sobbing day and night and failing fast.

Reaching home, I was shocked at the change in Mother.

She would not speak to me but seemed broken-hearted. My distress was very great. Could it be God's will for me to break my mother's heart?

At last one day as I listened to her pacing her bedroom floor, weeping, I could bear the strain no longer and determined to find out God's will. Going down to the parlor where the large family Bible rested on a desk, I stood for a moment crying to the Lord for some word of light. Then I opened the Bible at random, and the first words my eyes lit on were: "Ye have not chosen Me, but I have chosen you, and ordained you, that ye should go and bring forth fruit."

I knew at once God was speaking His will to me through these words, and in an instant the crushing burden was gone. Running to Mother's room, I begged her to hear what I had to say. Unwillingly she unlocked the door and stood while I told her of my prayer and answer. For a moment she hesitated, then she threw her arms about me, saying, "O my child, I can fight against you, but I dare not fight against God."

From that moment till her death, Mother's heart was entirely with me in the life I had chosen.

19

Find a Verse and Put Your Name in It

The upbringing and education of missionary children is both exciting and exacting. On one hand, few people are more fortunate than missionary kids. They grow up as internationals, the world their home, at ease as polyglots. They roam across Europe or explore Africa as easily as other children go around the block. On the other hand, many missions settings do not offer adequate schooling or needed interaction with other youth.

Ruth Bell Graham vividly remembers September 2, 1933. She was thirteen. Her father, a missionary surgeon in China, and her mother were sending her to boarding school in what is now Pyongyang, North Korea. For Ruth, it was a brutal parting, and she earnestly prayed she would die before morning. But dawn came, her prayers unanswered, and she gripped her bags and trudged toward the riverfront. She was leaving all that was loved and familiar: her Chinese friends, the missionaries, her parents, her home, her memories. The *Nagasaki Maru* carried her slowly down the Whangpoo River into the Yangtze River and on to the East China Sea.

A week later she was settling into her spartan dormitory. Waves of homesickness pounded her like a churning surf. Ruth kept busy by day, but evenings were harder, and she would bury her head in her pillow and cry herself to sleep, night after night, week after week. She fell ill, and in the infirmary she read through the Psalms, finding comfort in Psalm 27:10—*Even if my father and mother should desert me, you will take care of me.*

Still, the hurt and fear and doubt persisted. Finally, in desperation, she went to her sister Rosa, also enrolled in Pyongyang. "I don't know what to tell you to do," Rosa replied matter-of-factly, "unless you take some verse and put your own name in it. See if that helps." Ruth picked up her Bible and turned to a favorite chapter, Isaiah 53, and put her name in it: "He was wounded and crushed because of Ruth's sins; by taking our punishment, he made Ruth completely well."

Her heart leaped, and the healing began.

20

The Day of Trouble

Jamie Buckingham's book *Into the Glory,* tells the story of the Jungle Aviation and Radio Service, known as JAARS, the "flying arm of Wycliffe Bible Translators." He begins his account with missionary aviator Ralph Borthwick who was transporting a team of Gospel workers into the mountainous jungles of Peru. When Borthwick took off from the Wycliffe base in Yarinacocha, the weather was fine and the weather reports favorable. But suddenly, almost without warning, he was swallowed up by the worst storm he had ever seen.

Curtains of water cascaded over the plane, leaking in around the canopy and panels of the fuselage. Turbulence shook the little, single-engine amphibian so hard it seemed the rivets would pop out. There was nothing but static on the headset, and the rain got worse, like someone turning on a firehose to the windshield.

Borthwick felt as if he were in a submarine rather than an airplane as water spewed in from every seam and crack, drenching both him and his instrument panel. Then came hail, beating against the windshield like bullets. At the worst moment, the engines failed. Apart from the pounding rain and howling wind, there was nothing but silence. The droning of the engines had stopped.

As Borthwick struggled to retain control of the aircraft, he suddenly remembered the verse he and his wife had read just the day before at their breakfast table—Psalm 50:15: "Call upon Me in the day of trouble; I will deliver you, and you shall glorify Me."

During all the time of his emergency, Ralph realized he had not yet called on God. Now, with death seemingly only seconds away, he began to pray: "Father, if You still have work for me and my passengers, please bring on the engine."

At once, he thought of something. He had not yet pulled the little handle that would shut off outside air to the engine, the carburetor heat. He tried to dismiss the thought, for that wasn't something one would normally do in an emergency. But the thought came to him with force, and he reached down and jerked the carburetor heat handle, at the same time pulling back on the stick.

With a mighty roar the engines screamed to life. Borthwick shouted "Praise the Lord!" and, at literally the last second, he pulled his plane out of the dive. Ralph Borthwick lived to fly again.

In 1812, Adoniram and Ann Judson sailed from Massachusetts as America's first foreign missionaries. Then ended up in Burma where they suffered many heartaches and privations. On one occasion when Adoniram was imprisoned and sent far away, Ann followed with their children. She found her husband imprisioned in an old building without a roof, chained to other prisoners, and almost dead.

She herself had nowhere to stay, but the jailer allowed her and the children to share the tiny hut where he lived with his family. For six months, Ann lived in these primitive and almost hopeless conditions. Then she caught smallpox. Just as she was recovering from that, she contracted one of the tropical diseases that were almost always fatal to foreigners. She became so weak she could hardly walk, but with her last ounce of strength she set out for a nearby village to obtain medicine. She returned in a state of extreme weakness and exhaustion.

Shortly thereafter she contracted spotted fever and could not move. During this time her husband was placed in another obscure prison where she couldn't find him, and even the food she sent him was returned. She later wrote:

If I ever felt the value and efficacy of prayer, I did at this time. I could not rise from my couch. I could make no efforts to secure my husband. I could only plead with that great and powerful being who has said, "Call unto me in the day of trouble and I will hear, and thou shalt glorify me." God made me at this time feel so powerfully this promise that I became quite composed, feeling assured that my prayers would be answered.

The power of that verse carried Ann Judson through her darkest hours. If you're in storm or sickness today (even just in a little turbulence) remember Psalm 50:15: "Call upon Me in the day of trouble; I will deliver you, and you shall glorify Me."

21

Moody's Best Friend

Someone once asked evangelist Dwight Moody how he managed to remain so intimate in his relationship with Christ.

He replied, *I have come to Him as the best friend I have ever found, and I can trust Him in that relationship. I have believed He is Savior; I have believed He is God; I have believed His atonement on the cross is mine, and I have come to Him and submitted myself on my knees, surrendered everything to Him, and got up and stood by His side as my friend, and there isn't any problem in my life, there isn't any uncertainty in my work but I turn and speak to Him as naturally as to someone in the same room, and I have done it these years because I can trust Jesus.*

22

No Other Way

Civil war erupted in the Congo (Zaire) in the 1960s, and among the missionaries caught in the crossfire was a small sunbeam named William McChesney with Worldwide Evangelization Crusade (now WEC International). Though only five-foot-two, one hundred and ten pounds, Bill had an outsized personality that radiated cheer wherever he went. His co-workers dubbed him "Smiling Bill."

On November 14, 1964, suffering from malaria, Bill, twenty-eight, was seized by Congolese rebels. Despite ill treatment, violent sickness, and constant threats of death, his cheerful attitude didn't abandon him during captivity. A Catholic Nun who saw him during that time said, "That man has the face of an angel." Others said he seemed "utterly other-worldly." He sought every opportunity to witness to his captors.

Shortly afterward he was beaten mercilessly, his clothing ripped off, and he was thrown into a filthy, crowded cell which he shared with British missionary Jim Rodger. Catholic priests gave him their garments, for he was shaking violently from malarial fever.

The next day, November 25, Bill and Jim were dragged from their cell and forced to stand before a rebel colonel. At his command, the rebels fell on Jim and Bill with clubs and spears. Bill's death was almost instantaneous and Jim caught his body as it fell to the ground. The rebels then trampled Jim to death, and their bodies were thrown into the Wamba River.

Before leaving for Africa, Bill had written a poem explaining his desire for overseas missions.

I want my breakfast served at eight,
With ham and eggs upon the plate;
A well-broiled steak I'll eat at one,
And dine again when day is done.

I want an ultramodern home
And in each room a telephone;
Soft carpets, too, upon the floors,
And pretty drapes to grace the doors.

A cozy place of lovely things,
Like easy chairs with inner springs,
And then I'll get a small TV—
Of course, "I'm careful what I see."

I want my wardrobe, too, to be
Of neatest, finest quality,
With latest style in suit and vest:
Why should not Christians have the best?

But then the Master I can hear
In no uncertain voice, so clear:
"I bid you come and follow Me,
The lowly Man of Galilee."

If he be God, and died for me,
No sacrifice too great can be
For me, a mortal man, to make;
I'll do it all for Jesus' sake.

Yes, I will tread the path He trod,
No other way to please my God;
So, henceforth, this my choice shall be,
My choice for all eternity.

23

One in Seven

In the early days of the Nazi domination of Europe, the British Parliament still insisting on taking their weekends for leisure. Britain's ruling class left London for their country estates and didn't want to be bothered. It created no small problem, for crucial decisions could not be made in crisis because those in authority were unavailable.

Winston Churchill, frustrated beyond words, complained that Britain's rulers continued "to take its weekends in the country, while Hitler takes his countries in the weekends."

I've often thought of that when wishing more of our church members would take the Lord's Day more seriously. According to a recent poll, only 60% of all born-again Christians are in church on any given Sunday. Forty percent are AWOL.

When we neglect God's business on Sundays to pursue our own leisure, it gives Satan a free hand. Our bodies and souls are supposed to work six days and to rest on the seventh. We cannot persistently violate that law without breaking down at some point—either physically, emotionally, or in family relationships.

The British statesman William Wilberforce once jotted this in his journal about two political friends who had committed suicide: "With peaceful Sundays, the strings would never have snapped as they did from over-tension."

"Our great-grandparents called it the holy Sabbath," said one observer. "Our grandparents called it the Lord's Day. Our parents called it Sunday. And we call it the weekend."

Someone else wrote, "One generation called it a holy day; the next, a holiday; to the next, it was a hollow day."

I once heard Leslie Flynn likened the Sabbath to seven unmarried brothers who lived together in a large house.

Six went out to work each day but one stayed home. He had the place all lit up when the other six arrived home from work. He also had the house warm, and most importantly, had a delicious, full-course dinner ready for his hungry brothers.

One day the six brothers decided that the one that had been staying home should go to work. "It's not fair," they said, "for the one to stay home while the others slaved at a job." So they made the seventh brother find work too. But when they all came home the first night, there was no light, nor was there any warmth, and worst of all, there was no hearty dinner awaiting them. And the next night the same thing: darkness, cold, hunger. They soon went back to their former arrangement.

"[It's] the day of rest and worship that keeps the other six bright, warm, and nourishing," said Flynn. "When we desecrate the Lord's Day, we only hurt ourselves."

24

Not a Single Soul

Allen Francis Gardiner grew up in a Christian home, took to the sea, and achieved a successful British naval career with little thought for God. But in 1822, he fell ill and re-evaluated his life. He scribbled in his journal: *After years of ingratitude, unbelief, blasphemy, and rebellion, have I at last been melted? Alas, how slow, how reluctant I have been to admit the heavenly guest who stood knocking without!*

He was converted, and he soon began thinking about missions. Traveling around the world had given Captain Gardiner a glimpse of the need for missionaries, and he gave himself for the task. Leaving England for South America, he hoped to minister among the Araucanian or Mapuche Indians of Southern Chile. Government interference and inter-tribal fighting forced him back to England. Three years later he was at it again, visiting the Falklands and investigating the possibility of taking the gospel to the islands of Patagonia and Tierra del Fuego. Sensing opportunity at hand, Gardiner returned to England and on July 4, 1844, established a small organization called the Patagonian Missionary Society. He wrote, *I have made up my mind to go back to South America and leave no stone unturned, no effort untried, to establish a mission among the aboriginal tribes. While God gives me strength, failure will not daunt me.*

Gardiner visited South America a third time, but his efforts were again thwarted by inter-tribal fighting and governmental interference, the land being strongly Catholic, intolerant to Protestant missions. He returned to England, recruited six missionaries, and set sail for Tierra del Fuego. But all seven men died of disease, starvation, and exposure on Picton Island. Gardiner, the last to die, dated his final journal entry September 5, 1851: *Good and marvelous are the loving kindnesses of my gracious God unto me. He has preserved me hitherto and for four days, although without bodily food, without any feelings of hunger or thirst.*

Captain Allen Gardiner died without seeing a single soul saved among those for whom he was most burdened. But he lit a fire which has never gone out. His South American Missionary Society (as it came to be called) has been sending missionaries and saving souls for over one hundred and fifty years. ❧

25

Cosmos, Not Chaos

After a century of lambasting creationism, increasing numbers of scientists are admitting that the complexities of the cosmos cannot be explained apart from intelligent design.

I recently read a monograph by Dr. Owen Gingerich, professor of astronomy and the history of science at Harvard University and a senior astronomer at the Smithsonian Astrophysical Observatory. Gingerich referred to his friend, Fred Hoyle, a highly respected scientist of the first caliber, but an atheist. Hoyle discovered the remarkable nuclear arrangement of the carbon atom which is so uniquely and perfectly designed that if its composition and resonance level had been altered in the slightest way, life would be absolutely impossible.

Dr. Gingerich heard a rumor that Fred Hoyle had said that nothing had shaken his atheism as much as his discoveries regarding the carbon atom. But in their discussions together, Dr. Gingerich never mustered the courage to ask Dr. Hoyle if he had really said that.

Then Dr. Gingerich read this in an article by Fred Hoyle appearing in a Cal Tech publication: "Would you not say to yourself, 'Some supercalculating intellect must have designed the properties of the carbon atom, otherwise the chance of my finding such an atom through the blind forces of nature would be utterly minuscule.' Of course you would. . . . A common sense interpretation of the facts suggests that a superintellect has monkeyed with physics, as well as with chemistry and biology, and that there are no blind forces worth speaking about in nature. The numbers one calculates from the facts seem to me so overwhelming as to put this conclusion almost beyond question."

Dr. Owen Gingerich observed, "Fred Hoyle and I differ on lots of questions, but on this we agree: a common sense and satisfying interpretation of our world suggests the designing hand of a superintelligence."

Then Gingerich said this: "For me, it makes sense to suppose that the superintelligence, the transcendence . . . has revealed itself through the prophets in all ages, and supremely in the life of Jesus Christ. . . . [And] just as

I believe that the Book of Scripture illumines the pathway to God, so I believe that the Book of Nature, with its astonishing details like the resonance levels of the carbon atom, also suggests a God of purpose and a God of design. And I think my belief makes me no less a scientist."*

The Psalmist agreed when he wrote three thousand years ago, "The heavens declare the glory of God; And the firmament shows His handiwork." Believing that makes us no less intelligent—and a good deal wiser—than the scientific pundits of our age.

*Owen Gingerich, "Dare a Scientist Believe in Design?" *Evidence of Purpose,* ed. John Marks Templeton (New York: Continuum, 1994), 24–26.

26

A Dangerous Position

James Chalmers was a carefree, high-spirited Scottish boy. "I dearly loved adventure," he later said, "and a dangerous position was exhilarating."

Perhaps that's why he listened carefully one Sunday when his minister read a letter from missionaries in Fiji. The preacher, tears in his eyes, added, "I wonder if there is a boy here who will by and by bring the gospel to the cannibals." Young James said quietly, "I will!"—and he wasn't even yet converted.

In 1866, having been converted and trained, he sailed for the South Pacific as a Presbyterian missionary. Chalmers had a way with people. "It was in his presence, his carriage, his eye, his voice," a friend wrote. "There was something almost hypnotic about him. His perfect composure, his judgment and tact and fearlessness brought him through a hundred difficulties." Robert Louis Stevenson, who didn't like missionaries until he met Chalmers, said, "He is a rowdy, but he is a hero. You can't weary me of that fellow. He took me fairly by storm."

In 1877, Chalmers sailed on to New Guinea. His ministry was successful there. Packed churches replaced feasts of human flesh. But as the years passed, he grew lonely. He was delighted when young Oliver Tomkins came to join him in 1901. The two men decided to explore a new part of the islands, and on Easter Sunday they sailed alongside a new village. The next morning, April 8, 1901, Chalmers and Tomkins went ashore. They were never seen again. A rescue party soon learned that the men had been clubbed to death, chopped to pieces, cooked, and eaten.

News flashed around the world. "I cannot believe it!" exclaimed Dr. Joseph Parker from the pulpit of London's famous City Temple. "I do not want to believe it! Such a mystery of Providence makes it hard for our strained faith to recover. Yet Jesus was murdered. Paul was murdered. Many missionaries have been murdered. When I think of that side of the case, I cannot but feel that our honored and nobleminded friend has joined a great assembly."

God loves carefree, high-spirited youngsters who have a hankering for adventure. You never know what He may do with them. ❧

27

Finding What Mama Found

Dr. Doren Edwards, a surgeon in Erin, Tennessee, is a popular Gideon speaker who has visited our church on several occasions. Of all his stories, my favorite has to do with of a patient of his named Blanche Bennet whose alcoholic husband had died. Her two children were giving her problems, finances were tight, and life was very hard. She wasn't a Christian.

One day she came to see Dr. Edwards with physical problems, and he diagnosed cancer, with multiple organs involved. No treatment was available, and she was very bitter. Dr. Edwards, a Christian and a Gideon, wanted to talk with her about the Lord, but she wouldn't allow him to share his witness. She did, however, accept a small New Testament.

A few weeks later, the doctor learned from the newspaper obituary that she had died. He sent a card to the family, telling them he had donated Bibles in her memory to the Gideons.

The woman's daughter called him. "Could you please send us a Bible like the ones you donated in memory of our mother," she asked. "We don't have a Bible in our home. The last six days she was alive, her whole life changed. She was no longer bitter, she wasn't afraid to die, and she said something about knowing Jesus. But she asked that her Bible be buried in her hand, and we couldn't keep it. Would you please send us a Bible so that we can find what Mama found in that book?"

Dr. Edwards sent them a Bible, and to date the daughter, the son, and one sister have been saved as a result.

28

To Their Own Border

John and Edith Bell, missionaries in the western regions of China, were caught in the Japanese invasion of China during World War II. It was a brutal time, and a deep horror seized Edith when she learned that the couple's three children, far away in boarding school in Chefoo, had been seized and imprisoned at Weihsien Concentration Camp.

Edith went to the Lord in anguish, begging for His protection. In response, God gave her two special verses to reassure her heart—Jeremiah 31:16–17: "Thus says the Lord: 'Refrain your voice from weeping, And your eyes from tears; For your work shall be rewarded,' says the Lord, 'And they shall come back from the land of the enemy. There is hope in your future,' says the Lord, 'That your children shall come back to their own border.'"

One day a man arrived on the Bell's doorstep claiming to have contacts in the area around Weihsien, and he had good news. The children were alive and well cared for. They had adequate food and clothing.

Some time later, he came again, but his message was very different. "Mrs. Bell," he said, "I have some very sad news. All the students in the Weihsien Camp have been murdered."

Edith's mind reeled, and she fought to stave off total panic. Suddenly she remembered Jeremiah 31:16–17.

Grabbing her Chinese Bible, she quickly turned to those verses and said to the man, "Doctor, you read this." He read the words: "Thus says the Lord: 'Refrain your voice from weeping, And your eyes from tears; For your work shall be rewarded,' says the Lord, 'And they shall come back from the land of the enemy. There is hope in your future,' says the Lord, 'That your children shall come back to their own border.' "

Suddenly he threw down the Bible in disgust and stormed from the house. As it turned out, he was an infiltrator, trying to destroy the Christians' morale with lies.

Sometime later, John and Edith had to flee China, traveling westward through India. They eventually booked passage to America without knowing the condition of their children. As they disembarked in New York, a Red Cross worker greeted them with news their children had been liberated and had arrived back in Canada ahead of them.

"I was completely overcome," Edith said. "My children not only came from the land of the enemy, they came to their own border as the verse in Jeremiah had promised."

The Bells caught the next train to Ontario where "we stepped down and were almost knocked over by our three children. It was joy unspeakable and full of glory. God's 'I wills' had not failed, and we knew they never would."

29

Toothpicks and Orange Juice

The Tower of London, sitting forbiddingly on the Thames, is a small village within impregnable walls. It has served as a palace, a fortress, and, more ominously, a prison. Here a young Catholic named John Gerard suffered for his faith during the reign of Protestant Queen Elizabeth I.

He was a Jesuit priest, educated on the continent, who began covertly performing priestly work in England at age eighteen, moving from place to place one step ahead of the law. He was eventually captured and taken to the Clink, a prison so infamous that its name lives to this day. For three years he was kept there, sometimes chained, often attempting to escape. Then he was moved to the Tower of London.

One of the buildings there, the White Tower, contains a deep vault without windows or outer doors. There in the eerie glow of flickering torches, Gerard was hung by his hands for hours, day after day. When he fainted, he was revived and the torture reapplied. His arms swelled monstrously, his whole body throbbed, his bones screamed, and his hands became so damaged he couldn't even feed himself.

The torture was finally suspended for awhile. The young priest did finger exercises, and within three weeks he could again feed himself. Soon he asked for oranges and toothpicks. The toothpicks became pens. Orange juice became ink, visible only when heated. He began plotting his escape, smuggling out his invisible messages on notes to friends.

As messages flew back and forth, a rope, a boat, and outside helpers were recruited. On October 5, 1597, Gerard climbed through a hole to the roof of Cradle Tower, threw a rope over the side, and slid down it, wincing as it mutilated his hands. Friends whisked him to a hiding place outside London.

He was soon back at his clandestine priestly work, always a mere step from recapture. Finally it became untenable for him to stay in England, and he sadly slipped out of the country in the retinue of the Spanish and Dutch ambassadors, escaping to Italy. He labored in Rome until July 27, 1637, when he passed away at age seventy-three. He is known today as one of an elite handful of people who outwitted the Tower of London.

You and I may have meager resources, perhaps only toothpicks and orange juice. Perhaps only five smooth stones. Perhaps only a small lunch of five loaves and two fish. But don't discount God-given ingenuity, the power of a determined spirit, and a little help from on High. ❧

30

A Brief History of Rescue Missions

For the last one hundred years, urban-centered rescue missions have offered a gleam of hope for society's most downtrodden. Here the homeless and destitute can find a clean bed, a plate of food, a cheerful word, and a message of hope.

America's first rescue mission was started by Jerry McAuley, who was born in Ireland in 1839. His father, a counterfeiter, fled home to escape the law, and Jerry never knew him. His mother evidently languished in prison, and the boy was raised by his grandmother. When she couldn't control him, he was sent to New York to live with his sister, an arrangement that didn't last very long.

Jerry, incorrigible, fell into a life abandoned to

drunkenness and crime. He lived under the docks, drinking, fighting, and stealing from boats. He became one of the most despised ruffians on the lower east side, in and out of jail.

"Stealing came natural and easy," he later said. "A bigger nuisance and loafer never stepped above ground." In 1857, New York authorities had had enough, and at age nineteen, Jerry McAuley was sentenced to Sing-Sing, a dreaded prison on the east bank of the Hudson, thirty-three miles from New York.

As he stepped through the gateway, Jerry saw the sign reading, "The way of the transgressor is hard." It was a message new inmates quickly learned. Sing-Sing was a hideous prison. Prisoners were forced to live in unbroken silence in cell blocks five tiers high. Each cell was a little windowless coffin—three feet wide, six feet high, seven feet long. Sunshine seldom reached them. It was wet in the summer, icy in winter, always grim. There was no plumbing—just buckets—and the odor was sickening. Cells, never disinfected, filled with vermin, lice, and fleas. Infractions were punished by flogging, the "iron collar," or the "shower bath" in which prisoners were repeatedly drowned and revived.

For the first couple of years, McAuley tried to be a

model prisoner, but his attitude finally broke, and the resulting infractions brought punishments and additional hardships. He descended into ever-deepening despair.

One Sunday McAuley was herded into the chapel. He was moody and miserable until he glanced on the platform and recognized a well-known prize fighter, Orville Gardner. The boxer told of finding Jesus, and McAuley listened attentively. He soon began reading the Bible, page after page, day after day. He read it through twice; then in great agony he fell to his knees—but jumped up immediately in embarrassment. He did this several times.

Finally one night, resolving to kneel until he found forgiveness regardless of what anyone might think, he fell to his knees, and there he prayed and prayed. *All at once it seemed something supernatural was in my room. I was afraid to open my eyes; the tears rolled off my face in great drops, and these words came to me, 'My son, thy sins, which are many, are forgiven.'*

Rising to his feet, Jerry clapped his hands and shouted, "Praise God! Praise God!" His years of fighting and drinking were not over, but he had turned a corner and Jerry always afterward pointed to this moment as his conversion to Jesus Christ.

He was released in 1864, having been incarcerated seven of his twenty-six years. The Lord brought some Christians into his life who taught him the Scriptures, helped him find employment, and counseled him in overcoming his vices.

One day while working as a porter, Jerry found himself singing and worshipping God in a basement. Suddenly he had a sort of vision in which he sensed God calling him to engage in a special ministry to down-and-outers. As he later described it: "I had a sort of trance or vision. . . . I had a house and people were coming in. There was a bath and they came in and I washed and cleansed them outside and the Lord cleansed them inside. They came at first by small numbers, then by hundreds, and afterwards by thousands."

In October of 1872, he took possession of a building on Water Street in New York City and began a ministry to those who lived as he had once lived. For the next twelve years he was instrumental in winning thousands to Christ. When he died in September, 1884 (of tuberculosis contracted while at Sing-Sing), it seemed that all of New York City turned out for his funeral.

Today McAuley's New York City Rescue Mission stands at 90 Lafayette Street in Downtown Manhattan, not very far from its original wood frame building at 316 Water Street. It was the first of hundreds of rescue missions across America that have brought thousands into the kingdom.

There may be one in your community. If so, I'll bet it could use some prayer, a few volunteer hours, and a check in the collection plate.

31

Holy Ground

Wherever we are in our vocation, if Jesus is Lord of our lives, that place is a holy place of service for Him.

In January, 1995, J. Robert Ashcroft had fewer than forty-eight hours to live, but he was holding on to life, hoping to see his son, John Ashcroft, sworn into the U.S. Senate the following day. As family and friends gathered in Washington for a small reception, J. Robert Ashcroft asked his son to play the piano while everyone sang, "We Are Standing on Holy Ground."

After the song, the frail old man spoke some powerful words: "John, I want you to know that even Washington can be holy ground. Wherever you hear the voice of God, that ground is sanctified. It's a place where God can call you to the highest and best."*

*Adapted from Gary Thomas, "Working for All It's Worth," *Moody Magazine*, July/August, 1998, p. 13.

"The time of business," said the old mystic Brother Lawrence, "does not with me differ from the time of prayer, and in the noise and clatter of my kitchen, while several persons are at the same time calling for different things, I possess God in as great tranquility as if I were upon my knees at the blessed sacrament."

When we live in Christ's presence, we are always on holy ground. ❧

32

God's Man

As a young man growing up in rural North Carolina, George Washington Truett wanted to be an educator. Then a lawyer. All the while, his friends and fellow church members thought he should go into the ministry. Whenever he spoke to groups or taught Bible classes, his gifts of preaching and evangelism seemed evident to everyone but himself.

When his family moved to Whitewright, Texas, in 1889, George went with them and joined a local Baptist church where he was soon elected superintendent of the Sunday School. On several occasions he filled in for the pastor, but he always stood in front of the pulpit, explaining, "I will speak for Christ, but I am not worthy to be His minister."

Finally the church called a special business meeting on a Saturday night, and George was shocked to discover its purpose. The oldest deacon stood up and said, "I move that this church ordain Brother George W. Truett to the full work of the gospel ministry."

Truett tried to object, but he was outvoted. He later said, "There I was, against a whole church, against a church profoundly moved. There was not a dry eye in the house . . . I was thrown into the stream, and just had to swim."

A few years later, in September, 1897, Truett, now thirty years old and well-known, was named pastor of the First Baptist Church of Dallas. Some of his men, wanting to get to know him, took him quail hunting. Among them was Jim Arnold, the city's chief of police.

Another of the men later recounted what happened:

At 3:30 just as we were starting home, George Truett accidentally shot Capt. Arnold in the right leg, below knee, making an awful wound. I succeeded in stopping the blood by using my suspenders as a tourniquet. Brother Truett was in agony unspeakable. Never saw the like. Arnold suffers much. Fainted several times.

The following Sunday, Arnold died. All Dallas was stunned and Truett was devastated. He paced the floor day and night, unable to eat or sleep, muttering, "I will never preach again. I could never again stand in the pulpit."

Finally Psalm 31:15 came to his mind with vivid force: "My times are in Your hands." As he paced, he began mumbling, "My times are in thy hands. My times are in thy hands." Finally he collapsed in sheer exhaustion.

That night he vividly dreamed of Jesus standing by his bed. The Lord said, "Be not afraid. You are my man from now on." Later the dream came again, then a third time. At length it was announced that Truett was returning to the pulpit. Churches across Dallas dismissed services and gathered at First Baptist in support.

"When Brother Truett came into the pulpit," a member later said, "he looked terrible, his face drawn, his eyes sad. He remained silent for a long moment. You could have heard a pin drop. When he began, somehow he sounded different. His voice! I shall never forget his voice that morning . . ."

Truett remained at the First Baptist Church until his death in 1944. During his tenure he preached seventeen thousand sermons, membership increased from seven hundred to over seven thousand, with a total of 19,531 new members received and over five thousand baptisms recorded.

He was God's man now.

33

The Power of a Courteous Husband

Jay Kesler was once working at a Youth For Christ Camp in Ohio when a young woman approached him. They sat down in the front row of the chapel, and through many tears she told him her heartbreaking story. She had been molested by her own father about three times a week since she was four years old. She'd never told anyone about this, but had carried a great sense of secret shame. As they talked, Kesler noticed that both her wrists were scarred, and she admitted that she had tried to kill herself.

"Why didn't you do it?" Jay asked.

"Well," she replied, "I got to thinking . . . we have a youth pastor at our church . . . ."

At that point in the conversation, Kesler groaned within himself, thinking he was going to hear an ugly story about her getting involved with some youth pastor. But that wasn't it at all. She said, "He'd just gotten married before he came to our church, and I've been watching him. When he's standing in line in church behind his wife, he squeezes her right in church. They look at each other, and they hug each other right in church. One day I was standing in the pastor's study, looking out the window, and the youth pastor walked his wife out into the parking lot. Now there was only one car in the parking lot; nobody was around; nobody was looking. And that guy walked all the way around the car and opened the door and let her in . . . ."

Kesler thought to himself, "This is a nice story, but what's the point?"

But she continued: "Well, I just got to thinking that all men must not be like my dad, huh?"

"You're right," said Jay. "All men are not like your father."

"Jay, do you suppose our youth pastor's a Christian?"

"Yes, I think he probably is."

"Well, that's why I came tonight. I want to be a Christian, too."*

*Adapted from Jay Kesler, *Ten Mistakes Parents Make with Teenagers* (Brentwood, Tenn: Wolgemuth & Hyatt, Publishers, Inc.), pp. 29–30.

34

The Boy Preacher

Fifteen-year-old David Marks, eyes blurred with tears, left home with a dollar in his pocket to preach the gospel. The "boy preacher" soon created a stir in the American northeast, and he kept going for the next twenty-five years, becoming one of the most powerful preachers in early American history. He rode one horse nineteen thousand miles, preached to thousands, organized Freewill Baptist churches throughout New England, published books, wrote articles, taught school, and worked diligently in opposition to slavery and in support of foreign missions.

Marks preached one of his most unusual sermons just before sunset on May 13, 1828. He had ridden into the little town of Ancaster, Ontario, announcing he would preach in seven minutes in the park. A small crowd gathered, and he asked if anyone had a text he would like to hear preached. A man mockingly said, "Nothing!"

Marks immediately began preaching on *nothing*. God created the world from *nothing,* he said. God gave us laws in which there is *nothing* unjust. We have broken God's law and there is *nothing* in us to justify us. There will be *nothing* to comfort sinners in death or hell. But, while we have *nothing* of our own in which to boast, we have Christ. And He gives *nothing* to cause us grief, *nothing* to disturb our peace, and *nothing* to fear in eternity.

Finishing his sermon, Marks mounted his horse and traveled to the next village. But some time later he returned to Ancaster. This time a larger group assembled, and the meeting house was opened to him. David preached *something* to them. He said there is *something* above all things. There is *something* in man designed to live forever, but there is also *something* in us that makes us unhappy. There is *something* about the gospel that reverses our unhappiness, *something* that gives us hope. There is *something* that will disturb the impenitent in death, but *something* resides in Christians that the world can't understand, and *something* in eternity to give us everlasting joy.

All that from an uneducated young circuit-rider, his mind filled with Scripture and his heart full of Christ, who had something to say—and nothing to fear.

Years passed. On November 18, 1845, David Marks, was forty years old and dying, having utterly exhausted himself from his tireless labors. He had one more unusual sermon up his sleeves. Though he was on his deathbed, he asked his friend Charles Finney, if he could address the students of Oberlin College.

Marks' friends tried to dissuade him, but he was insistent. He was carried to the college and Finney announced him to the startled students, warning them that Brother Marks would probably not survive his sermon. He said Dr. Dascomb could find no pulse in one wrist, and only "a little tremulous motion" in the other. If he should die while preaching, the students were to remain calm and not leave their seats.

Thus introduced, Marks began his last sermon. His text was Micah 2:10. He said:

My dear friends, I thank God that I have the prospect of addressing you once more, and for the last time. This has been the desire of my heart. The lamp of life has for some time been flickering in its socket, and in the opinion of friends

I have but a few hours to live. I suppose my coffin is being made.

My extreme weakness, and the distress of suffocation in consequence of the dropiscal difficulty in my chest, and which is probably drowning my heart, has not allowed me to spend a moment in preparation for this meeting. Hence my remarks must be made offhand. The first and leading thought of which I wish to dwell is that God has not designed this place as our final home. As the prophet said, "Arise and depart, for this is not your rest. . . ." The light of a blessed immortality dawns beyond the tomb. Christ is so near and so precious that I cannot fear death. O, my brethren, no reality is so sure, none so sweet, none so glorious, as the Christian's hope. . . .

He spoke of the brevity of life, the certainty of heaven, then he ended by urging the students, *O live for God and your generation! You enter life at a glorious time to live—there is so much to do for God. Farewell. Brother Finney, I want to give you my hand. All of you who love God, farewell.*

None of the students ever forgot that dramatic sermon. Marks was carried back home where he shortly "arose and departed" to his rest.

35

"I Wasn't Addressing You, Mr. President"

There is a story that when Bill Moyers was a special assistant to President Lyndon B. Johnson he was once asked to say grace before a meal in the family quarters of the White House. As Moyers began praying softly, the President interrupted him with "Speak up, Bill! Speak up!"

Moyers, a former Baptist minister from east Texas, stopped in mid-sentence and without looking up replied steadily, "I wasn't addressing you, Mr. President."

When we're talking with God, even presidents are "small potatoes."

36

Where Is the Lord God of Elijah?

Seven young men sailed to a small island off the coast of mainland China to evangelize the fishing village of Mei-hwa. It was the 1920s, and the group was led by a promising young evangelist named Watchman Nee, later to become one of China's most powerful Christian leaders. It was a pagan village, but at least one Christian lived there, a midwife, the surrogate mother of one of the young men. It was she who had asked them to come.

Despite intense effort, the young men didn't see the slightest results to their witnessing. The villagers ignored them. Finally the youngest of the evangelists, Kuo-ching Lee, shouted to a crowd in frustration, "What's wrong with you? Why don't you believe?"

"Oh, we do believe," came back a reply. "We believe in our great king, the god Ta-Wang. He never fails us."

As Kuo-ching questioned the crowd, he learned that every year the village staged a great festival for their god, Ta-Wang. For the last 286 years it had not rained on that annual festival day. And as it turned out, the celebration was only two days away, on January 11. Impulsively Kuo-ching Lee announced, "Then I promise you, our God, who is the true God, will make it rain on the eleventh."

The crowd took up his challenge. "Say no more," they replied. "If there is rain on the eleventh, then your Jesus is indeed God. We will be ready to hear Him."

When Watchman Nee heard about the exchange he was deeply troubled, and he started to rebuke Kuo-ching Lee for his rashness. But instead he stole away for a time of prayer. "Father, have we gone too far?" he asked. "Should we leave this village now before Your Name is maligned? Should we turn these people over to themselves?"

Instantly a phrase from 2 Kings 2:14 came to his mind: *Where is the Lord God of Elijah?* Watchman Nee thought of the contest between Elijah and the prophets of Baal on Mount Carmel, recorded in 1 Kings 18. He began wondering if God intended to do something similar in the village of Mei-hwa. The next day during his prayer time the same verse returned to his heart with unusual tenacity: *Where is the Lord God of Elijah?*

Convinced that God intended to perform a miracle on the eleventh, Watchman instructed his young men to broadcast the challenge throughout the area. The Lord God of Elijah would send rain on January 11, a day that had not seen a drop of rain in almost three centuries.

The news spread quickly, and everyone in the village became caught up in the excitement of the contest. It was the subject of every conversation.

When January 11 dawned, it was a perfect day. The sun rose in a cloudless sky, and Watchman Nee had to shield his eyes from its brightness. The villagers, assured that Ta-Wang was the true god after all, scurried about preparing for their festival. Deeply disturbed, Watchman began to pray, "Lord, this doesn't look like the rain that You . . . ." Suddenly his prayer was interrupted by 2 Kings 2:14: *Where is the Lord God of Elijah?*

Quickly dressing, Watchman joined his companions at the breakfast table. As they bowed their heads over the food, he offered a simple blessing: "Father, please accept our prayer as a gentle reminder that You promised to answer the challenge of the demon-god today. Even though not a cloud appears in the sky, we trust in Your promise."

Before Watchman pronounced the "Amen," the seven young men heard a few drops hitting the tiled roof. As the rain began falling, villagers hurried to protect their false god, hoisting him onto a platform to be carried down the street. As they started off, the rain fell in sheets, then in a torrential downpour. Water rose in the streets until it reached the porches of many houses, and as the false priests tried to carry their heavy statue, they slipped in the deluge, and their idol crashed to the pavement, breaking its arm and head.

When the storm finally abated, the pagan priest quickly repaired the idol and announced he had made a grave mistake. The annual celebration, he said, was to have fallen, not on January 11, but on January 14.

"Lord," Watchman Nee prayed, "give us good weather until that hour. We have much to do." During the next three days, the seven young men evangelized around the clock, and thirty villagers confessed Christ as Lord.

When the revised day arrived, exactly at the appointed hour, another mammoth storm hit Mei-hwa. From that moment, paganism's hold on the island was broken. A church was established. And the faith of seven young men was dramatically strengthened for their years of ministry to come.

37

Walking

Christians are living witnesses who should walk worthy of the calling they have received. We are to:

- Walk before Him and be blameless—Genesis 17:1
- Walk in His statutes—Leviticus 26:3
- Walk in all His ways—Deuteronomy 10:12
- Walk uprightly—Psalm 84:11
- Walk in newness of life—Romans 6:4
- Walk by faith and not by sight—2 Corinthians 5:7
- Walk in the Spirit—Galatians 5:16
- Walk in love—Ephesians 5:2

In her biography of Marie Antoinette, Carolly Erickson tells about the queen's attempts to disguise herself and attend parties, dances, and balls incognito, but her walk gave her away. "When she walked, she strode like a man. Her swift, purposeful gait was her trademark. It was said that she could never successfully disguise her identity at masked balls, for no matter how she dressed, she still walked like an Empress."

F. W. Boreham reminds us of a story from the life of Francis of Assisi. "Brother," Francis said one day to one of the young monks at the Portiuncula, "let us go down to the town and preach!"

The novice, delighted at being singled out to be the companion of Francis, obeyed with alacrity. They passed through the principal streets; turned down many of the by-ways and alleys; made their way out to some of the suburbs; and at length returned, by a circuitous route, to the monastery gate. As they approached it, the younger man reminded Francis of his original intention.

"You have forgotten, Father, that we went down to the town *to preach!*"

"My son," Francis replied, "we *have* preached. We were preaching while we were walking. We have been seen by many; our behavior has been closely watched; it was thus that we preached our morning sermon. It is of no use, my son, to walk anywhere to preach unless we preach everywhere we walk."

38

The Prodigal

One of the most powerful personal evangelists of the nineteenth century was "Uncle" John Vassar, who grew up in his family's brewery in Poughkeepsie, New York. Following his conversion to Christ, he abandoned beer-making for soul-winning, and on May 15, 1850, he was commissioned as an agent for the American Tract Society of New York. Vassar took off across the country, never resting in his mission of selling Christian literature and asking everyone he met about their relationship with Christ.

On one occasion, traveling in the West, he visited the home of a praying wife whose husband was an infidel. She begged for a Bible, and Vassar gave her one and went his way. He had no sooner left when the husband, coming home, saw the book and was enraged. Seizing the Bible with one hand and the ax with the other, he hurried to the wood-pile where he placed it on the chopping block and hacked it crosswise in two. Returning to the house, he threw half of the destroyed Bible at his wife, saying, "As you claim a part of all the property around here, there is your share of this."

The other half he tossed into his tool shed.

Months later on a wet winter's day, the man, wanting to get away from his Christian wife, retreated to his shed. The time passed slowly, and in boredom he looked around for something to read. Thumbing through the mutilated Bible, his attention was caught by the story of the prodigal son in Luke 15. He became absorbed in the parable only to discover that its ending belonged to his wife's section. He crept into the house and secretly searched for the bottom half of the book but was unable to find where his wife had hidden it.

Finally he broke down, asked her for it, and read the story again and again. In the process he came to the Heavenly Father like a penitent prodigal returning home.

39

"Little Is Much If God Is in It"

I do not believe there are any small churches," Joseph Parker once wrote. "I am more and more convinced that we should be very careful what epithets we attach to the term *church.*" Many people have struggled with the idea that their church is not growing quickly enough. Here are some men who overcame those fears:

In their book, *Liberating Ministry from the Success Syndrome,* Kent and Barbara Hughes describe their anguish when, early in ministry, they were given a promising church-planting work in Southern California. When the work floundered, Kent grew depressed. "If church attendance was up, I was up; if it was down, so was I. And the numbers had been going down for a long time."

Gradually, the Lord led the Hughes to ponder these

questions: "Can a man be a success in the ministry and pastor a small church? What is failure in ministry? What is success in ministry?"

From the experience, Kent learned that God defines success in ministry as being faithful, serving others, loving and trusting Him, praying, pursuing holiness, and developing a positive attitude.

This liberating discovery enabled Hughes to plunge back into his work, despite its paucity, with joy and enthusiasm. "We saw how success was equally possible for those in the most difficult situations . . . as well as those having vast ministries."

After the Civil War, the great Baptist leader John Broadus, burdened for more preachers to heal the nation's wounds, prepared a course on preaching techniques for ministerial students at Southern Seminary. To his dismay only one student, a blind man, enrolled in the class.

"I shall give him my best and I shall pursue my lectures as planned," said Broadus. Day after day, Broadus gave his lectures conversationally to his solitary, sightless student—lectures so powerful they later became the classic, *The Preparation and Delivery of Sermons,* that has gone though countless printings and is inspiring young ministerial students to this day.

On September 14, 1898, at the Central Hotel of Boscobel, Wisconsin, John Nicholson arrived at 9 P.M., longing for a quiet room to write up his orders. To his disappointment, every room was taken. The clerk suggested he share room nineteen with a stranger, Samuel Hill.

Before crawling into bed, Nicholson opened his Bible. At age twelve, he had promised his dying mother he would read the Bible every night at bedtime. "Read it aloud," said Hill, "I'm a Christian, too." Nicholson read John 15, and the two knelt for prayer. Then they stayed up till 2 A.M. discussing the spiritual needs of Christians on the road.

Nicholson and Hill bumped into each other again the following May in Beaver Dam, Wisconsin. They soon announced plans for an association of Christian salesmen and set the first meeting for July 1, 1899. Only three showed up—Nicholson, Hill, and Will J. Knights. The men nonetheless launched their organization to mobilize Christian commercial travelers for encouragement, evangelism, and service. They groped for a name, but after they had prayed about it Knights said, "We shall be called Gideons." The Gideons have since distributed over seven hundred and fifty million copies of Scripture in over one hundred and seventy nations.

George Matheson grew discouraged over his small crowd one winter's evening in Innellan, Scotland. He had worked hard on his sermon, but the sparse numbers and empty chairs nearly defeated him. He nevertheless did his best, not knowing that in the congregation was a visitor for the large St. Bernard's Church in Edinburgh, which was seeking a pastor.

"Make every occasion a great occasion," said Matheson, who was to spend the rest of his career at St. Bernard's. "You can never tell when somebody may be taking your measure for a larger place."

Many people don't know that the most far-famed pastor in British history, Charles Spurgeon, was converted on a Sunday when a blizzard kept everyone away from church except a tiny handful. Not even the preacher showed up that day, but an old fellow, a common laborer, finally tried to preach a few words. It was a miserable effort in human terms, and he perhaps went home thinking the day a failure. He didn't know he had just won to Christ a boy who would preach six hundred times before he was twenty years old, who would become the most popular preacher in London, whose collected sermons would fill sixty-three volumes (which is the largest set of books by a single author in the history of Christianity), and whose every sermon would instantly sell twenty-five thousand copies and be translated into twenty languages.

Carl S. Dudley wrote, *In a big world, the small church has remained intimate. In a fast world, the small church has been steady. In an expensive world, the small church has remained plain. In a complex world, the small church has remained simple. In a rational world, the small church has kept feelings. In a mobile world, the small church has been an anchor. In an anonymous world, the small church calls us by name.*

40

Never Mind

Once, just as an oratorio of his was about to begin, several of George Frideric Handel's friends gathered to console him about the size of the audience. Not many people showed up.

"Never mind," Handel replied. "The music will sound the better" due to the improved acoustics of a very empty concert hall.

Somehow that reminds me of another story.

Once, when an acquaintance praised Johann Sebastian Bach for his wonderful skill as an organist, he replied with characteristic humility and wit: "There is nothing very wonderful about it. You have only to hit the right notes at the right moment and the instrument does the rest."

Humility, it seems, is that rare virtue that makes us clever, gracious, well-liked, self-assured—and sometimes funny.

41

Water Wars

Charles Bowles' father was African; his mother was the daughter of a Revolutionary War hero. He was converted as a youth and called to the Freewill Baptist ministry. On July 24, 1816, he preached his first sermon, and his ministry soon resulted in both converts and controversy. He was a black preacher in the far north, making waves and winning souls. In Huntington, Vermont, a mob secretly plotted to attack him at his next worship service. They intended to tie him to a wooden horse and plunge him in the lake to sink or swim as he would. Bowles, however, heard of the plot.

His biographer later wrote: *The time arrived for the meeting; and while the enemy was preparing the weapons of their warfare, he is fitting himself. Behold him in yonder grove, bowed low before the throne of the Redeemer. What a noble sight to behold that despised servant of God, bowed alone in the grove, seeking only a preparation of heart! What a contrast with that band preparing by whiskey and oaths.*

The service began, and the mob, seated before him, awaited its signal. Bowles read Matthew 23:33—*You are nothing but snakes! How can you escape going to hell?* He preached with such fervor that no one dared move. He finished by saying, "I am informed there are persons here who have agreed to put me on a wooden horse, carry me to the pond, and throw me in; and now, dear creatures, I make no resistance." But he had one request—that on the way to the lake the assembly sing hymns. "Glory be to God! Yes, we will have music. Glory to God!"

This was said with his powerful voice with such confidence in God that it went like an electric shock through the congregation, and produced an effect upon the mob that could scarcely have been equaled had a bolt from heaven fallen; so completely were they overcome, that they fell prostrate upon the floor.

Shortly afterward, the troublemakers did meet Bowles at the lake—where *he* plunged *them* into its chilly waters, baptizing them as followers of his Lord Jesus.

42

Fret Not

In one of his books, Methodist pastor Charles Allen tells of visiting a particular city. Being met at the plane, he was told, "We don't have time to wait for your baggage. Someone else will get it. You are to speak at the club in twenty minutes." Rushing from the airport, Allen learned he was to speak each morning on television at nine, at church at ten, and somewhere else each evening. He was also to address three civic clubs, two high schools, and one women's meeting. In all, he had nineteen speaking engagements in four days—plus a series of personal interviews.

By Wednesday night Allen found himself wound so tightly he scarcely slept a wink. The worries and pressures got to him.

The next day he rebelled. After the morning engagements . . . *I told the pastor I would be gone for the remainder of the day. I started walking slowly down the street, going no place in particular and in no hurry to get there. A number of people spoke to me and stopped and talked awhile. It reminded me of living in a little town where you can enjoy visiting up and down Main Street.*

I walked on past the city limits until I came to a big bridge on the river. I found a comfortable place to sit down and I sat there for two hours watching the river . . . . From the bridge I could see the point where two rivers flowed together. One of the rivers was almost clear, the other extremely muddy. For a short distance after they came together, you could distinguish the water of each, but a little farther on the clear water took on the brownish color of the other. I thought about how we let evil thoughts come into our minds and how the evil soon colors all our living. I made some mental notes for a sermon about that.

At the end of the bridge was a tiny hamburger place. I had one with onions; in fact, I asked for an extra onion. It tasted real good. I didn't care whether or not it left an odor on my breath. I had been so pious all that week that I was in the mood to do something daring.

I walked along the street until I came to a cemetery . . .

[and] spent an hour walking among the graves. During that hour I was the only person there. I thought about how quickly someone is forgotten and how others take our places. It is not so important that we carry the world on our shoulders as we sometimes think.

I got back to the hotel for dinner before the preaching service that night. I felt rested and relaxed. When I got back to my room after the service, I went to bed. I picked up my Bible from the table and opened it to the Thirty-seventh Psalm. Next to the Twenty-third, that is my favorite Psalm. It was written for people who get disturbed and overly wrought-up.

*The Thirty-seventh Psalm is gentle and tender; like a sweet kindly mother putting her hand upon the brow of a restless child, the Psalm begins, "Fret not thyself . . ." It goes on to say, "Delight thyself also in the Lord; and he shall give thee the desires of thy heart." Further on we read, "Rest in the Lord, and wait patiently for Him . . ." All the way through, the Psalm leads one to a calm and triumphant faith. That night I slept easily, and the next day I felt rested and strong.**

We weren't made for a nonstop, twenty-four-hour, frantic pace. We need to take time for ourselves, time to relax, time to walk by the still waters, time waiting before the Lord, for there alone can we renew our strength and overcome worry. ❧

*Charles L. Allen, *Prayer Changes Things* (Westwood, NJ: Fleming H. Revell Co., 1964), pp. 62–64.

43

Only Fourteen

Missionary Christine Tinling once visited a leper colony in Foochow, China, where she heard of an old man who had showed up one day asking for a room in which to die. He wore only a bit of burlap tied by a few strings. He had no relatives, but the Christians took him in and loved him like their own.

One day the Chinese pastor visited the old man and began sharing the gospel, but when the pastor asked him if he wanted to become a Christian, he said "No. Jesus gave himself to me, but I have nothing to give him in return for a gift like that."

"But he wants no gift except yourself," said the pastor. It took awhile for the old man to comprehend this. He kept asking, "How could he possibly want an ill-smelling, rotten old leper like me?" But finally one day he believed and received Jesus as Savior.

The man quickly learned to love the Word of God and he began sharing Christ with fellow lepers, going from room to room, until the disease caused his feet to drop off and his eyes to fall out.

As he lay dying, his one regret was that he had done so little for the Lord. He had learned the gospel too late, when he was hardly able to move about. Looking up at his pastor, he asked this question: "When I reach Father's house, will Jesus blame me for not getting any more, or will he remember I was just a rotten old leper?" Then he added: "I only got fourteen."

Fourteen souls he had won to Jesus Christ.

On the resurrection day, said Christine Tinling in recounting the story, *from a grave outside Foochow will rise this child of God, who, in the days of his flesh, was a leper and an outcast. He will have his own place in the blessed company of whom it is written: "They will be Mine in that day when I make up my jewels."*

44

Smoking the Bible

Jacob Koshy grew up in Singapore with one driving ambition: to be a success in life, to gain all the money and possessions he could. As a young man, he discovered crime and the underworld as his fast track to success. Soon he was deeply involved in the world of drugs and gambling, and eventually he became a one-man international smuggling network.

In 1980 he was caught, arrested, and placed in a government drug rehabilitation prison in Singapore. It was more than he could bear. All his goals, purposes, dreams, and ambitions were locked up with him in a tiny cell, and his heart was full of a cold, sterile emptiness that frightened him.

Jacob was a smoker, and cigarettes weren't allowed in the center, so he smuggled in tobacco and rolled it in the pages of a Gideon Bible which he tore out one at a time, as needed. One day he fell asleep while smoking. He awoke to find that the cigarette had burned out, and all that remained was a scrap of charred paper. He unrolled it and read what was written: "Saul, Saul, Why do you persecute me?"

Jacob became so curious about the quote that he asked for another Bible and read the entire story of the conversion of Saul of Tarsus. He suddenly realized that if God could help someone like Saul, God could help him, too. There in his cell he knelt and prayed, asking Christ to come into his life and change him. He began crying and couldn't stop. The tears of a wasted life washed away his pain, and God redeemed him.

As Jacob started sharing his story with the other prisoners, he found them attentive. As soon as he was released, he became involved in a church. He met a Christian woman, married, and became a missionary in the Far East where he tells people far and wide, "Who would have believed that I could find the Truth by smoking the Word of God?"

45

The Lonely President

Brutal, bare-fisted political scandals are nothing new to American politics. Andrew and Rachel Jackson were vilified by their critics and the press during his presidential campaigns. Rachel had previously married Army Captain Lewis Robirds, but he proved an abusive husband, and the marriage was unhappy. She separated from him and believed she had successfully obtained a divorce.

The Jacksons were married in Natchez, Mississippi, only to learn two years later that Rachel's divorce was not properly processed. Andrew and Rachel were remarried on January 17, 1794, in Nashville. They loved each other very deeply, and, though both were stubborn and strong-willed, they were a devoted and tender couple.

In the 1828 presidential campaign, Jackson's opponents dug up some information about Rachael's previous marriage and used it against her husband, making this one of the most bitter contests in American history. Andrew was called a "paramour husband," and Rachel was labeled a "convicted adulteress." Out of his deep devotion to his wife, Jackson lashed back in anger. Rachel meanwhile suffered inwardly and withdrew to their home, the Hermitage, outside Nashville. Being a devout Christian, she turned to her Bible for comfort.

Jackson won the election and rejoined Rachel at the Hermitage to prepare for their move to Washington. But it wasn't to be. On December 22, 1828, on the eve of their much heralded departure for the nation's capital, Rachel wasn't feeling well. She dreaded their move to the White House, and her overweight condition added to her feelings of fatigue. As her maid Hannah helped her to a chair by the fire, Rachel remarked, "I would rather be a door-keeper in the house of God than to live in that palace."

Twenty minutes later, she cried, "I am fainting!" and collapsed in Hannah's arms. The servant's screams brought Andrew bursting into the room, followed by doctors and friends. Rachel was lifted into bed as the doctors listened for her heartbeat. There was none.

Andrew was so ravaged in grief that friends feared he, too, might succumb.

But a few days later, having buried his beloved, the grim but determined President-elect left alone for "that palace" at 1600 Pennsylvania Avenue, arriving there lonelier than any of its occupants before or since.

Andrew Jackson himself didn't become a Christian until near the end of his life. For years he had heard the gospel message from some of America's strongest preachers, including Peter Cartwright. But Jackson told friends that he didn't want to convert to Christianity while still engaged in politics for fear some would think he was doing it to win votes or curry favor.

But in July, 1838, after his political career was over, Old Hickory rode across the field to Tulip Grove Presbyterian Church, which he had help build years before for Rachel, and there he made a formal profession of faith in Jesus Christ. He explained that the hardest thing about becoming a Christian was forgiving his enemies. Yet he said he could and would forgive his enemies.

But, he added, Rachel's enemies remained for God to deal with.

46

Failure?

Peter Marshall, revered chaplain of the United States Senate, once quipped, "It is better to fail in a cause that will ultimately succeed, than to succeed in a cause that will ultimately fail." John F. Kennedy gave us a good illustration of that in his award-winning *Profiles in Courage*.

Kennedy told of George W. Norris of Nebraska, who began his career as a country teacher on the plains of Nebraska. Then he became a small-town lawyer, a local prosecuting attorney, and then a judge. In 1903, he entered the House of Representatives, and he was later elected to the senate. Kennedy describes him as a "chunky figure" clothed in "drab black suits, white shirts, and little shoestring ties."

Norris was an independent-thinking Republican who sometimes took up unpopular causes and fought uphill battles, saying, "I would rather go down to my political grave with a clear conscience than ride in the chariot of victory."

Interestingly, he lost many of his most anguishing political fights. But years later, looking back over his life and career, Norris made this observation to a friend: *It happens very often that one tries to do something and fails. He feels discouraged, and yet he may discover years afterward that the very effort he made was the reason why somebody else took it up and succeeded. I really believe that whatever use I have been to progressive civilization has been accomplished in the things I failed to do rather than in the things I actually did do.*

The Scottish author Samuel Smiles put it this way: "It is a mistake to suppose that men succeed through success; they much more often succeed through failures. Precept, study, advice, and example could never have taught them so well as failure has done."

47

One Surviving Book

Alexander Duff, first foreign missionary of the Church of Scotland, got off to a rough start. He was young, only twenty-three, and bright and innovative. But on his way to India in 1829 with his new wife, he was shipwrecked—not once but twice! The most serious wreck occurred when his ship, the *Lady Holland,* was within a few miles of India.

At 10 o'clock at night Duff was half-undressed when a shock and shudder ran through the vessel. He rushed to the deck where the captain met him with terrifying words, "Oh, she's gone! She's gone!" The ship split apart, but a portion clung precariously to a reef. Through the night the passengers huddled in terror in the surviving portion, expecting every moment to be swept away. They were saved the next day, but their clothes and prized possessions were lost, including Duff's entire library of eight hundred volumes.

Later, standing on the shore and looking sadly toward the reef, Duff saw a small package bobbing atop the water. He watched and waited as it floated close enough for him to wade out and retrieve.

It was his Bible. Of all his precious books, it alone survived. His heart soared, for he took it as a sign from the Lord that this one book alone was worth more than all the others put together.

He assembled his fellow survivors and read Psalm 107, the Traveler's Psalm. Soon, using the same Bible, he began his first class with a little group of five boys under a banyan tree. Within a week the class had grown to three hundred, and it soon became a school that evangelized and educated the higher classes in India, producing a qualified generation of leaders for the nation's young church.

48

Be Careful Little Eyes

While traveling in Europe recently, my wife and I were disturbed that the television sets in our hotel rooms were programmed to show a fleeting second of raw pornography as we flipped through the channels. The hotel hoped to snare us into paying to see the whole video.

The corrupting power of a flash of entertainment is nothing new. In the fourth century, the famous St. Augustine had a student named Alypius with whom he developed a mentoring relationship. Alypius, though not yet a Christian, sought a virtuous life, and, accordingly, he detested the entertainment of his day—the gladiatorial games of the Roman Empire. The thought of pitting humans against each other or against vicious animals was, to Alypius, revolting.

But one day Alypius chanced upon a group of fellow students who coerced him to the amphitheater. “Though you drag my body to that place and set me down there,” Alypius protested, “you cannot force me to give my mind or lend my eyes to these shows. Thus I will be absent while present, and so overcome both you and them.”

The Coliseum soon became a tumult of inhuman frenzy. Alypius sat with his eyes squeezed tightly shut, forbidding his mind to gaze upon the scene of moral wickedness surrounding him. But he couldn’t close his ears, and when one of the combatants fell in the fight, a mighty cry rose from the multitude. Overcome by curiosity, the youth opened his eyes for just a moment, and the drama of the games shot into his mind like a sword.

Augustine later wrote, “As soon as he saw the blood, he drank in with it a savage temper, and he did not turn away, but fixed his eyes on the wicked contest. . . . He was no longer the same man who came in. . . .” Alypius was instantly addicted to this evil, and that is the way he lived until long afterward, when both he and Augustine were converted to the Lord Jesus Christ.

It all reminds us of the little children’s song:

Be careful, little eyes, what you see.
Be careful, little eyes, what you see.
For the Father up above
He is looking down in love,
So, be careful, little eyes, what you see.

49

That Kind of Stuff

Sometimes the best way to deal with temptation is to rule it out in advance. According to Harry Truman's biographer, David McCullough, President Truman was under incredible pressure while attending the Potsdam Conference. He was not only meeting with Churchill and Stalin; it was in Potsdam that he ordered the use of the atomic bomb against Japan.

One evening near the end of an arduous session at the palace, Truman prepared to leave for his nearby lodgings. A young Army public relations officer, seeing Truman about to leave in his car, stuck his head in the window and asked to hitch a ride. Truman told him to get in, and the two struck up a conversation, overheard and later reported by Truman's driver.

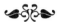

In Berlin the black market was rampant, and everything was available—cigarettes, watches, whiskey, and prostitutes. The officer said that if there was anything the President wanted, anything at all he needed, he had only to say the word. "Anything, you know, like women."

Truman, who was deeply devoted to his wife Bess and wrote her love letters almost every day, bristled. "Listen, son, I married my sweetheart," he said. "She doesn't run around on me, and I don't run around on her. I want that understood. Don't ever mention that kind of stuff to me again."

Truman's driver later recalled, "By the time we were home, he got out of the car and had not even said goodbye to that guy."

The best way to resist temptation is, whenever possible, evade it. Just say "No," before the question is asked. Make up your mind before the occasion arises. The only thing better than being rescued from quicksand is avoiding it to begin with. As the Bible puts it in Romans 13:14: "But put on the Lord Jesus Christ, and make no provision for the flesh, to fulfill its lusts."

50

Our Hearts Are Restless Until . . .

"You stand here and watch the world go by, don't you?"

I had ducked into a newsstand at Chicago's O'Hare for a paper, and the small, gray-haired lady who took my money had perceptive eyes and oversized glasses. She only glanced at me, her attention barely leaving the mass of humanity that was coming and going in a blur of motion. I was intrigued by her absorption in the flowing crowd, so I ask her, "You just stand here and watch the world go by, don't you?"

"Yes . . ." she said, her eyes still on the humanity. "Yes, and much of it is sad."

She turned briefly to me, gave me my change and my paper, and nodded toward the men's bathroom across the concourse. "You wouldn't believe the suicides they take out of that washroom. Many men go in there and kill themselves, and the paramedics take them out one after another, all the time."

With that observation, she dismissed me from her attention, her eyes transfixed again by humanity.

The great Israeli statesman, Abba Eban, wrote in his autobiography about a conversation he once had with Edmund Hillary, the first man to climb Mount Everest. Eban asked Hillary what exactly he felt when he reached the peak. He replied that the first sentiment was one of ecstatic accomplishment. But then there came a sense of desolation. What was there now left to do?

In May, 1996, journalist Jon Krakauer was part of an expedition that reached the top of Mount Everest. Twelve of his compatriots were killed in the highly publicized descent, a story that Krakauer records in his book *Into Thin Air.* But he begins his account by describing his feelings on May 10, 1996, as he reached the highest spot on earth:

Straddling the top of the world, one foot in China and

the other in Nepal, I cleared the ice from my oxygen mask, hunched a shoulder against the wind and stared absently down at the vastness of Tibet. I understood on some dim, detached level that the sweep of earth beneath my feet was a spectacular sight. I'd been fantasizing about this moment, and the release of emotion that would accompany it, for many months. But now that I was finally here, actually standing on the summit of Everest, I just couldn't summon the energy to care . . . .

I snapped four quick photos . . . then turned and headed down. My watch read 1:17 P.M. All told, I'd spent less than five minutes on the roof of the world.

Tennis star Boris Becker said something similar: "I had won Wimbledon twice before, once as the youngest player. I was rich. I had all the material possessions I needed . . . . It's the old song of movie stars and pop stars who commit suicide. They have everything, and yet they are so unhappy. I had no inner peace. I was a puppet on a string."

"I'm shocked by the hole in America's heart," observed television producer Normal Lear. And Robert F. Kennedy, Jr. once wrote, "Everybody basically has an empty hole inside of them that they try to fill with money, drugs, alcohol, power—and none of the material stuff works."

What does work?

The French mathematician and philosopher Blaise Pascal wrote, "There is a God-shaped vacuum in the heart of every man which cannot be filled by any created thing, but only by God the Creator, made known through Jesus Christ."

Even earlier, in the fourth century, St. Augustine said, "Our hearts are restless until they find their rest in Thee."

Jesus said, "I have come that they may have life, and that they may have it more abundantly" (John 10:10).

51

This Is My Buddy

In *Guideposts Magazine* Donald Vairin of Oceanside, California, told of serving as a young hospital corpsman in the invasion of Guam during World War II. While navigating some dangerous waters, his boat hit a coral reef and came to a sudden, grinding halt. The commanding officer, realizing the ship was sinking, ordered everyone off at once.

Donald jumped into the ocean and sank like a rock, his carbine rifle, medical pack, canteen, and boots dragging him down. He forced himself to the surface, gasping for air, only to sink again. He tried to pull off his boots, but the effort exhausted him, and he began to sense he wasn't going to make it.

Just then he saw a man thrashing in the water next to him, and in desperation he clutched onto him. That proved enough to hold him up and get him to the reef where he was picked up by a rescue boat. But Donald felt so guilty about grabbing the drowning man to save himself that he never told anyone what had happened.

About six months later on shore leave in San Francisco, he stopped in a restaurant. A sailor in uniform waved him over to sit with him, and as he did so he announced to his friends, "This is my buddy. He saved my life."

"What are you talking about?" asked Donald.

"Don't you remember?" asked the man. "We were in the water together at Guam. You grabbed on to me. I was going down, and you held me up."*

In God's grace it sometimes happens that in receiving help, we somehow impart it also. That is friendship—people who need each other and, in clinging to one another in hard times, find unexpected mutual strength.

*Adapted from Donald Vairin, "His Mysterious Ways," in *Guideposts,* September, 1999, p. 39.

52

The Story Behind "Revive Us Again"

Here in his own words is the remarkable story of a Scottish medical doctor named W. P. Mackay, the author of the famous gospel song, "Revive Us Again."

My dear mother . . . had been a godly, pious woman, quite often telling me of the Savior, and many times I had been a witness to her wrestling in prayer for my soul's salvation.

But nothing had made a deep impression on me. The older I grew the more wicked I became. For the God of my mother I did not care in the least, but rather sought by all means to drive Him out of my thoughts. I was in danger of becoming a thorough infidel, but for the voice of my conscience ever accusing and reproaching me.

About this time an incident that crossed my life gave

it an entirely different course. One day a seriously injured (laborer) who had fallen a considerable distance while climbing a ladder was brought into the hospital. The case was hopeless; all we could do was ease the pains of the unfortunate man.

He seemed to realize his condition, for he was fully conscious, and asked me how long he would last. As it was in vain to keep the truth from him, I gave him my opinion in as cautious a manner as I could . . . .

"Have you any relatives whom we could notify?" I continued.

The patient shook his head. He was alone in the world. His only wish was to see his landlady, because he owed her a small sum, and also wished to bid her farewell. He also requested his landlady send him, "The Book."

"What book?" I questioned.

"Oh, just ask her for the Book, she will know," was his reply.

After a week of such suffering, he died. I went to see him on my regular visits at least once a day. What struck me most was the quiet, almost happy expression which was constantly on his face. I knew he was a Christian, but about such matters I cared not to talk with him or hear.

After the man had died, some things about the deceased's affairs were to be attended to in my presence.

"What shall we do with this?" asked the nurse, holding up a book in her hand.

"What kind of book is it?" I asked.

"The Bible of the poor man. His landlady brought it on her second visit. As long as he was able to read it, he did so, and when he was unable to do so anymore, he kept it under his bed cover."

I took the Bible and—could I trust my eyes? It was my own Bible! The Bible which my mother had given me when I left my parents' home, and which later, when short of money, I sold for a small amount. My name was still in it, written in my mother's hand. Beneath my name was the verse she had selected for me. I stood as if in a dream, but I regained my self-control, managing to conceal before those present my deep emotion. In seemingly indifferent manner and tone I answered the nurse, "The book is old and has hardly any value, let me keep it, and I will see about the rest."

I took the Bible to my room. It had been used frequently. Many leaves were loose, others were torn; the cover was also damaged. Almost every page gave evidence that it had been read very often. Many places were underscored, and while looking through it, I read some of the precious verses, and a word I had heard in the days of my youth came back to memory.

With a deep sense of shame I looked upon the Book, the precious Book. It has given comfort and refreshing to the unfortunate man in his last hours. It has been a guide to him into eternal life, so that he had been enabled to die in peace and happiness. And this Book, the last gift of my mother, I had actually sold for a ridiculous price.

I need not add much more. Be it sufficient to say that the regained possession of my Bible was the cause of my conversion.

It was this man, Dr. W. P. Mackay, who later wrote the famous hymn *Revive Us Again:*

Revive us again,
Fill each heart with Thy love
May each soul be rekindled
With fire from above.
Hallelujah! Thine the glory
Hallelujah! Amen.
Hallelujah! Thine the glory
Revive us again.

53

Loud and Clear

As a terrified, wide-eyed boy in the Philippines during World War II, Fred Magbanua saw terrible acts of carnage that no child should ever witness, and at times he wondered if there was hope in the world, either in life or beyond death.

After the war, searching for answers, he began listening to the broadcasts of the evangelistic short-wave radio ministry of Far East Broadcasting Company. There he heard the gospel, and at length Fred received Christ as his Savior. Having a penchant for technology and broadcasting, he entered the field of civil engineering and was hired by FEBC to work at their transmitting site in Manila.

In time, he became director of Far East Broadcasting Company, Philippines, and regularly read the Scripture over the radio and taught the Bible on air. He told his wife, Aliw, that he wanted to do nothing more than God's will. He was happy in the Lord's work.

But one day Fred received a letter offering him a lucrative engineering job in New York. He was immediately attracted to the money, but his wife was bothered. Had he not committed himself to work only for Christ? Why was his head being turned by promises of worldly advancement and money? She cautioned him to move slowly and prayerfully.

Ignoring his wife's uneasiness, Fred began dreaming of America. He impulsively decided it was an offer he couldn't refuse.

That night Fred's FEBC broadcast was from Romans 12:1–2. He recorded the program, then left the studios. Outside the building, he noticed a burned-out warning light atop the towering antenna and decided to change it at once. He threw the switch, not realizing the high voltage wasn't effectively grounded, and he climbed to the top of the three-hundred-foot tower.

Suddenly a powerful electromagnetic field of ten thousand watts of radio frequency current seized him and began burning him alive. He lost his hold as his hands flew into the air, and he dangled by his neck, writhing in pain, unseen in the night. Suddenly he was shocked to hear his own voice reading Romans 12:1: "I beseech you therefore, brethren, by the mercies of God, that you present your bodies a living sacrifice . . . ."

His own programming was going out over the antenna at that moment, and his head, locked by the radio frequency power, was acting as a conductor.

Fred lost consciousness, saying, "Lord, I commend to You my spirit," and his body toppled toward the ground. Miraculously he fell only eight feet before catching on a brace. A fuse blew, saving him from burning to death. But a dozen deep burns seared through his head to his skull, and x-rays showed a black spot on his brain. During three months hospitalization, Fred suffered indescribable pain. But as Christians around the world prayed, he recovered. He left the hospital determined to be the Lord's living sacrifice, and he has since served Far East Broadcasting Company for many years.

He had gotten the message loud and clear. ❧

54

Singing to Yourselves

In her *Dear Abby* newspaper column, Abigail Van Buren once shared a letter from R. T. Holland of Los Angeles who told of an article from the medical section of *Time* Magazine. The magazine cited a man who went to a psychiatrist complaining that he was always hearing radio broadcasts. Thinking to humor him, the psychiatrist asked what he was hearing right then. The man replied that he was hearing Rudy Vallee broadcasting from the Steel Pier in Atlantic City.

After much questioning he discovered that the man worked in a glass bottle factory and had gotten some silica crystals in dental cavities. The combination of the silica, saliva, and some bridgework in his mouth had literally transformed him into a walking crystal radio receiver!

The psychiatrist referred the patient to a dentist

who gave his teeth a thorough cleaning, filled the cavities, and fixed the bridgework. As a result, the patient "went off the air," was able to concentrate, and lived happily ever after.

The Bible says that those who are filled with the Spirit are tuned into the heavenly frequency and carry a song around with them everywhere they go—speaking to themselves in songs, hymns, and spiritual songs, singing and making music to the Lord in their hearts. As someone once put it, "The Christian life is simply God's life vibrating through us."

"I awakened yesterday morning," Edith Shaeffer once wrote in *Christianity Today,* "with music and words surging though my head: 'Great is thy faithfulness; great is thy faithfulness; morning by morning new mercies I see . . . .' It was as if a full orchestra and choir were in my room, yet no sound could be heard by anyone else. What a fantastic detail of God's creation—people can sing aloud, and can sing within . . . . We don't need to waken the whole household by bursting forth in song; we can rejoice in song in our heads at night, or start the day or the year that way."

Another Christian lived in a land where God's music was not allowed to be played. Every morning he took out his score on Handel's *Messiah* and placed it on the dining room table. Then, on the table, his fingers silently and diligently played through the entire score. He was making music that only God could hear.

And do not be drunk with wine, in which is dissipation; but be filled with the Spirit, speaking to one another in psalms and hymns and spiritual songs, singing and making melody in your heart to the Lord (Ephesians 5:18–19).

55

Smoking

When the name Billy Graham became nationally known, so many tourists showed up each day at the Graham home just outside of Asheville, North Carolina, that eventually the family purchased several acres of mountain land and built a log house where they could have some privacy. Since Billy was away preaching most of the time, Ruth oversaw the construction, taking along the couple's oldest child, Franklin, who was intrigued by the workers, their tools—and especially by their cigarettes.

"I caught on that if I ran quick enough when they pitched a cigarette," Franklin later recounted, "the butt would still be lit. I would grab one and puff away, thinking no one would notice."

But his mother would often notice, and would coming running over to grab the cigarette out of his mouth and lecture him on the evils of smoking. The workmen seemed to enjoy the sideshow, so they kept pitching half-smoked cigarettes in Franklin's direction. A bad habit began early.

One evening shortly afterward, in an effort to break Franklin of smoking, Ruth borrowed a pack of cigarettes, pulled one out, and handed it to Franklin. "Now light it and smoke it," she snapped, "and be sure to inhale." She wanted Franklin to get sick, hoping he'd lose his desire to smoke. After the second cigarette, his face turned green, and he ran to the bathroom and threw up. But he stubbornly came back for more, and by the end of the night he had finished all twenty.

The years passed, and one day in 1974 Franklin, now a young man, yielded his life at last to Jesus Christ. But one of the things that most surprised him following his commitment to Christ was discovering his taste for cigarettes as strong as ever. He genuinely wanted to quit smoking, but it proved nearly impossible. He later explained that he would wake up at night with "an absolutely overwhelming—almost terrifying—desire for a cigarette. I wanted to smoke so bad that I couldn't think of anything else. It intensified with each passing minute.

Throughout the day, the yearning for a cigarette grabbed me like the jaws of a junkyard dog."

He finally shared his struggle with his friend Roy Gustafson. "Roy, I quit smoking, but I don't think I can hold out. I just don't think I have the power to say no any longer."

"Oh, you don't, huh?" replied Roy, looking up from a hamburger. "Why don't you just get down on your knees and tell God He's a liar?"

"What? I can't do that!"

Roy quoted 1 Corinthians 10:13 to him: *No temptation has overtaken you except such as is common to man; but God is faithful, who will not allow you to be tempted beyond what you are able, but with the temptation will also make the way of escape, that you may be able to bear it.*

Then, looking at Franklin, he said bluntly, "You need to tell God He's a liar. You claimed that verse and it didn't work."

"I'm not going to call God a liar," said Franklin, alarmed. "Besides, I haven't claimed that verse yet!"

"You haven't?" said Roy, sounding shocked. "Why don't you, then?"

Franklin did claim that verse. And it did work.

56

Anywhere, Lord

V. Raymond Edman was long gone from Wheaton College when I arrived as a student there in 1975, but stories about him lingered, passed down from class to class. I remember hearing, for example, how Edman, as president of the college, would arise in the early morning hours, walk to each student dormitory, lift up his hands, and pray for God's blessings on the students that day.

I recall hearing of how he had advised and guided a young Wheaton student named Billy Graham into the ministry of evangelism.

Following his recovery from a heart attack in 1967, V. Raymond Edman, then chancellor of Wheaton, had returned to campus to preach in the chapel. Rising to the pulpit, he told the students he wanted to take them into the presence of the King of Kings. Then as the stunned student body watched in horror, he had slumped to the floor, dying instantly of another massive heart attack.

He left a mark behind him—circled, underlined, and highlighted. His contagious Christian influence as a missionary, pastor, and college president touched thousands of lives, and his writings on the "Victorious Christian Life" moved millions more.

Edman, born in Chicago in 1900, had never intended to be a college president. He had attended the University of Illinois and Columbia University, served in the U.S. Army in France and German, then shipped out to work among the Quichua Indians in the Andes of Ecuador. His life's goal was to be a missionary. But while in South America, he contracted a terrible tropical disease and his health broke.

Seeking to regain his strength, Edman took a Pacific voyage in 1928 aboard a Dutch freighter, the *Boskoop*. He missed his missionary work terribly, and even though his weakness made it hard to leave his stateroom, he labored intently over the lectures he hoped to give at his Ecuadorian Bible institute.

As he outlined the book of 2 Corinthians, he reached chapter two, and read the words, "Now thanks be to God who always leads us in triumph in Christ. . . ." He was staggered. He read the words several times, slowly, prayerfully, phrase-by-phrase.

He suddenly sensed a great contrast between that verse and his condition. Here he was, broken health, unsure future, anxious about his missionary service, not far from death's door. Yet to Paul, life was ongoing, unbroken triumph! Edman walked to the deck and began praying for a triumphant spirit. Quickly and quietly, the Lord seemed to whisper in his ear, "But are you willing to go anywhere for Me?"

Slowly, with trembling heart, Edman replied, "Yes, Lord, anywhere in Ecuador Thou mayst send me."

"I did not say in Ecuador."

For a long time, Edman gazed across the Pacific, conscious that the Lord was standing beside him, awaiting an answer. Finally in deepest sincerity, Edman replied, "Yes, Lord, anywhere Thou sayest I will go, only that my life may be always a constant pageant of triumph in Thee." He stood there for a very long time, thinking of the testimony of George Mueller who once told of the moment when he died to self, to ambition, to the praise or blame of men, only that he might live in Christ. Now he, too, had abandoned all—even his ministry goals—for the sake of Christ.

From that day, God began to use V. Raymond Edman in an unprecedented way, in raising up a young generation of Christian workers, equipping students, writing books, overseeing ministries, and preaching the realities of the Deeper Christian Life. His motto can be no less our own: Now thanks be to God who always leads us in triumph in Christ. ❧

57

No Hopeless Cases

Pictures of Mel Trotter (1870–1940) show a distinguished gentleman with serious face, slight smile, silver hair, wire glasses around perceptive eyes. His favorite verse was 2 Corinthians 5:17, and for good reason:

Therefore, if anyone is in Christ,
he is a new creation;
old things have passed away;
behold, all things have become new.

Trotter's father, a bartender, taught Mel the trade at an early age. Despite the earnest prayers of his mother, Mel followed his dad headlong into runaway drinking, smoking, and gambling. When he married, his habits reduced his family to poverty. Mel sold the family possessions from under his wife's nose to replenish his drinking money, then he resorted to robbery to satisfy the craving for more booze.

One day Trotter staggered home to find his young son dead in his mother's arms. Over the boy's casket, Mel promised to never touch another drop of liquor as long as he lived, a resolve that barely lasted through the funeral.

Shortly afterward, Mel, age twenty-seven, hopped on a freight car for Chicago. It was a bitterly cold January night, but he sold his shoes for some drinking money. After being evicted from a bar on Clark Street, he headed toward Lake Michigan to commit suicide. Somehow he ended up at the Pacific Garden Mission so drunk the doorman had to prop him against a wall so he wouldn't fall off his chair.

Despite his inebriation, at the close of the service Trotter raised his hand for prayer and trusted Christ as his Savior. The change was instant and remarkable. Mel Trotter became a new creation. Second Corinthians 5:17 became his testimony verse, and he began sharing it everywhere. His wife came to Chicago to join him, and in time Mel Trotter became one of the most sought-after preachers, speakers, soul-winners, and rescue workers in America.

"The greatest day I ever lived was the 19th of January, 1897," he once said, "when the Lord Jesus came into my life and saved me from sin. That transaction revolutionized my entire life. Don't call me a reformed drunkard. I am a transformed man, a child of God."

58

I Only Had an Hour

All I needed was a little peace and quiet—just an hour or so. Just a cup of coffee and time to think. And just a quiet spot. The fuss and flutter of the holidays had upset my schedule, and most of my tasks remained undone. The Christmas cards weren't in the mail; the gifts were unwrapped—most of them unpurchased—and holiday preparations at church were percolating.

Only careful, disciplined planning, I reasoned, would enable me to survive the season.

So I chose a little café that served European pastry and a variety of coffees. Its atmosphere was quiet, with soft classical Christmas music in the background. Patrons sat at bistro tables, reading novels or working on crossword puzzles. Here, I thought, I can spread out my calendar, make my "to do" lists, sip my coffee, and schedule the milliseconds between now and December 25.

I only had an hour.

But I no sooner entered the café than I heard a familiar voice. An old friend, Dan Cronk, having little to do that morning, had decided to enjoy a pot of tea and a basket of breads. There he stood, tray in hand, looking wistfully, delighted to see me and obviously hoping I'd invite him to sit down.

I didn't want him to join me, for he was a talker, able to rattle away for hours on hypothetical abstractions from his brilliant but rambling mind.

There he stood nonetheless.

"Well, hello Dan!" I said with a broad smile. "I didn't expect to see you here."

"Didn't have much goin' on this morning, and I thought a pot of tea would cheer me up. Meeting someone?"

"Well, no . . . Actually, I'm not . . . er . . . Want to join me?"

"Sure!"

And down he sat.

For the next hour I sat there, head nodding and stomach knotting, listening to him pour forth. My planning calendar rested unopened on the table, and my blood pressure slowly increased in steady increments. I silently cursed the impulse that had chosen *that* particular café on *that* particular day at *that* particular hour.

The hour passed, and I cleared my throat. "Well, Dan, it's been wonderful seeing you again. I have to go now, but I hope you have a wonderful Christmas."

He looked deeply into my eyes, and I noticed for the first time that his were soft, tender, vulnerable. He smiled and reached his hand across the little table and laid it atop mine.

"I'm so glad we ran into each other today," he said quietly. "Thanks for taking time for an old man. I was feeling pretty blue this morning, and I guess I just needed a friend. You know, sitting here with you has felt like . . . well, it's been like pulling up to a blazing fire on a cold night. I feel so . . . so warm now. Thanks for letting me join you."

That incident took place years ago, and Dan is now in heaven. But I've thought of his words many times since. They were so simple, yet the more I mull over them the more profound they seem. I'm always tempted to allow the holiday to deteriorate into nothing more than jingling bells and jangled nerves. Dan reminded me that Christmas isn't decorations, deadlines, and dashing through the snow. It's a time for giving ourselves—specifically, our *time*—to someone with greater needs than our own. And we do it in honor of the Baby who did the same for us, the one called "'Immanuel'—which means 'God with us'" (Matthew 1:23).

Time for friends and fellowship in Jesus' name.

It's like pulling up to a blazing fire on a cold and lonely night.

59

Tears

In Lou Holtz' second season as head football coach of the Notre Dame, the Fighting Irish experienced a humiliating loss against Texas A & M in the Cotton Bowl. Holtz slunk into the locker room shaken and depressed, but his blood pressure rose as he noticed that most of his players didn't seem very distraught.

The only exception was a second-string sub named Chris Zorich who was sitting in front of his locker sobbing. Holtz decided just then that next year's team would be composed of players who loved football as much as Zorich.

The next season this young man went from sub to starter to team captain and helped the Fighting Irish win a national championship.

Chris Zorich had won the spot on the starting team because of his tears, for some things are worth crying over.

"A tear," said Bible teacher M. R. DeHaan, "is a distillation of the soul. It is the deepest longing of the human heart in chemical solution."

Charles Spurgeon called tears "the diamonds of heaven."

The late Golda Meir, Prime Minister of Israel, said, "Those who don't know how to weep with their whole heart, don't know how to laugh either."

Gregg Levoy, writing in *Psychology Today,* reports that crying can actually remove chemicals that build up during emotional stress. According to Levoy, the amount of manganese stored in the body affects our moods, and the body stores thirty times as much manganese in tears as in blood serum. Biochemist William Frey says the lachrymal gland, which determines the flow of tears, concentrates and removes manganese from the body. Frey has also identified three chemicals stored up by stress and released by crying.

During their years as medical missionaries to China, Dr. and Mrs. L. Nelson Bell faced many challenges, including civil war, bandits, and Japanese occupations. But none was so difficult as the death of their infant son, little Nelson Bell, Jr.

In a letter dated 1925, Dr. Bell wrote:

Virginia and I realized that he was going, and we were with him alone when the end came. It was so sweet and so peaceful, no struggle and no evidence of pain, just quietly leaving us and going back to Him.

His going has left an ache in our hearts and our arms feel very empty, but oh the joy of knowing he is safe. It has but drawn us closer to Him and given us a new tie and joy to look forward to in heaven. We would not have him back for we know it was His will that he should go . . . .

Virginia expressed my feelings exactly as we were leaving the little cemetery (owned by the hospital) when she said, "I have a song in my heart, but it is hard to keep the tears from my eyes."

Allan Emery, successful business leader, has devoted much of his time to providing leadership to many Christian organizations. He is highly respected as a shrewd yet kind man. Credit his father.

Allan recalls taking a extended train trip as a youngster. One morning in the dining car, he heard his father, an important businessman, comment that the porter seemed to be in pain and walked with a limp. The poor man, it turned out, was suffering from an infected ingrown toenail.

Later in the morning, Allan was surprised to see the porter coming from his parent's sleeping car. There was a distressed look on his face, and as he passed by big tears fell from his eyes and cascaded down his cheeks. Going into the men's lounge, the man put his hands over his face and cried. Allan sat down on the bench beside him and at length asked, "Are you crying because your toe hurts?"

"No," said the man, "it was because of your daddy."

With great concern, Allan pressed for the story. His parents had returned from breakfast and immediately approached the porter, asking about his toe. Mr. Emery explained that he wasn't a doctor, but he might be able to help him. He removed the man's shoe and sock, and carefully lanced the infected toe, cleaned it, and carefully bandaged it.

"It doesn't hurt at all now," said the porter through his tears. "It feels fine."

"Then why are you crying?"

"Well, while he was dressing my toe, your daddy asked me if I loved the Lord Jesus. I told him my mother did but that I did not believe as she did. Then he told me that Jesus loved me and had died for me. As I saw your daddy carefully bandaging my foot, I saw a love that was Jesus' love and I knew I could believe it. We got down on our knees and we prayed and, now, I know that I am important to Jesus and that He loves me."

With that, the porter burst into tears again. When his sobs subsided, he looked over at Allan and said, "You know, boy, kindness can make you cry."

Have your eyes watered with tears recently? Somehow, in God's grace, it's all right. Somehow, in His sight, your tears are precious.

60

God's Image in Ebony

"Work hard at whatever you do," says Ecclesiastes 9:10. In the New Testament, Colossians 3:23 states a similar truth: "And whatever you do, do it heartily, as to the Lord."

Perhaps no one worked harder than Amanda Smith, who learned this trait from her father. Amanda was born into slavery in Long Green, Maryland, on January 23, 1837. She was one of thirteen children. Her father, Samuel Berry, belonged to one master, and her mother was owned by another master in the same town. Samuel worked tirelessly to earn enough money to purchase freedom for his children. He made brooms by day, then after dark he walked several miles to work in the fields until one or two o'clock in the morning. Returning home, he slept for an hour or two, then was up again.

In this way he eventually purchased freedom for every member of his family.

Although Amanda attended school for less than four months, she learned to read, teaching herself by cutting letters out of newspapers and forming them into words. At age thirteen, she went to work as a servant for a widow in York, Pennsylvania. While there, a revival broke out in a nearby Methodist Episcopal Church, and Amanda attended the services. "I was the only colored girl there, but I went," she later recalled. During one of the services, a young woman approached her, begging her to go forward. Amanda went, and the girl knelt with her, placing her arm around her and praying for her. Amanda went home that night resolving "to be the Lord's and live for Him."

Amanda labored in the kitchen with renewed vigor, earning a reputation for her Maryland biscuits and fried chicken. She also became known as the area's best scrub woman. She often stood at her washtub from six in the morning until six the next morning, then worked for hours at her ironing board. When overcome by fatigue, she would lean her head on the window ledge and sleep a few moments till the need passed.

In 1855, Amanda, in New York at the time, visited

the Green Street Methodist Episcopal Church to hear Rev. John S. Inskip preach. His sermon was from Ephesians 4:24: *Put on the new man which was created according to God, in true righteousness and holiness.*

"How long is a dark room dark when you take a lighted lamp into it?" asked Inskip. As he continued to preach, Amanda said she felt "the touch of God from the crown of my head to the soles of my feet." She didn't go forward at the invitation, because there were so many white people present she was afraid of causing a controversy. But as she later recalled, she left the service "with a touch of which I cannot describe. It seemed to press me gently on the top of my head, and I felt something part and roll down and cover me like a great cloak. It was done in a moment, and O what a mighty peace and power took possession of me."

Amanda became a powerful prayer warrior, and she constantly knelt in prayer, sometimes beside an old trunk or chair, or by a tree, or beside a fallen log. She called it "taking the knee route." She prayed when she hadn't enough to eat. She prayed to understand the Bible better, to be wiser in her ministry, and for her needs to be provided. She prayed when racial tension erupted around her, placing her in danger. Her attitude was that if a person doesn't have any problems or hardships, he has nothing to pray about.

She also began witnessing, and her power as an evangelist quickly gained notice. She began accepting invitations and was soon in demand as a Methodist holiness evangelist. She evangelized as far south as Knoxville, as far west as Austin, and as far north as Maine. She traveled alone by train and with simplicity, her belongings rolled in a carpetbag. Her fame leaped the Atlantic, and in 1876 she was called to England for meetings, then to India, then to Africa. In all, she served as an overseas missionary fourteen years, evangelizing on three continents.

Returning to America, she organized women's bands, young people's groups, temperance societies, children's meetings. And she started an orphanage near Chicago, the Amanda Smith Orphan's Home for Colored Children, financing it initially with proceeds received for her autobiography, *The Lord's Dealings with Amanda Smith.*

Though never ordained, she brought many to Christ through her preaching. She said, "The thought of ordination never entered my mind, for I had received my ordination from Him who said, 'Ye have not chosen Me, but I have chosen you, and ordained you, that you might go and bring forth fruit.'"

She died on February 24, 1915. She was called "God's image carved in ebony."

61

Abide with Me

Henry Francios Lyte was of delicate health all his life, but that didn't stop him from working like an ox, year after year, as he pastored faithfully among the seafaring folks around Devonshire, England. But finally his strength gave out, and in 1847 his doctor suggested he move to the milder climate of southern France.

It was a heartbreaking parting, and Lyte couldn't leave without one final sermon to his church of twenty-four years. His health was so frail, that his friends advised against it. But Lyte was determined. Standing feebly, he said, "Oh, brethren, I stand here before you today, as alive from the dead, if I may hope to impress upon you and get you to prepare for that solemn hour which must come to all. I plead with you to become acquainted with the changeless Christ and His death."

Finishing his sermon, he served the Lord's Supper to his weeping flock and dismissed them.

That evening as his life's work drew to its close, he found comfort in pondering John 15: "Abide in Me, and I in you . . . ." According to his gardener, Lyte then walked down to the ocean and watched the "sun setting over Brixham harbor like a pool of molten gold." Taking a piece of paper, he wrote out a poem, returning to his study to rewrite and polish it before handing it to his adopted daughter.

The next day he left for France. Reaching Nice, he had a seizure and passed away with the words, "Joy! Peace!" on his lips. His poem, however, lived on, becoming one of our most beloved hymns:

Abide with me—fast falls the eventide!
The darkness deepens—Lord, with me abide;
When other helpers fail and comforts flee,
Help of the helpless, O abide with me!

Hold Thou the cross before my closing eyes;
Shine thro' the gloom, and point me to the skies.
Heav'n's morning breaks, and earth's vain shadows flee!
In life, in death, O Lord, abide with me.

62

The Endless Chain

Edward Kimball, a Christian worker in nineteenth century Boston, was determined to win his Sunday school class to Christ. One of the boys, a teenager named Dwight Moody, tended to fall asleep on Sundays, but Kimball, undeterred, set out to reach him at work.

Kimball's heart was pounding as he entered the store where the young man worked. "I put my hand on his shoulder, and as I leaned over, I placed my foot upon a shoebox. I asked him to come to Christ." But Kimball left thinking he had botched the job. His presentation of the gospel seemed halting, and he was downcast. Moody, however, left the store that day a new person and eventually became the most prominent evangelist in America.

Years later, on June 17, 1873, Moody arrived in Liverpool, England, for a series of crusades. The meetings went poorly at first, but then the dam burst and blessings began flowing. Moody visited a Baptist chapel pastored by a scholarly man named F. B. Meyer who at first disdained the American's unlettered preaching. But Meyer was soon transfixed and transformed by Moody's message.

At Moody's invitation, Meyer toured America. At Northfield Bible Conference, he challenged the crowds saying, "If you are not willing to give up everything for Christ, are you willing to be made willing?" That remark changed the life of a struggling young minister named J. Wilber Chapman.

Chapman proceeded to become a powerful traveling evangelist in the early 1900s, and he recruited a converted baseball player named Billy Sunday. Under Chapman's eye, Sunday became one of the most spectacular evangelists in American history. His campaign in Charlotte, North Carolina, produced a group of converts who continued praying for another such visitation of the Spirit. In 1934, they invited evangelist Mordecai Ham to conduct a citywide crusade.

On October 8, 1934, Ham sat alone in his hotel room, dejected and discouraged. His evangelistic campaign in Charlotte was faltering, the newspapers were blasting him, the churches were fighting him, and he seemed powerless to go any good. Sighing deeply, he took a sheet of hotel stationary and wrote out this prayer:

Dear Father: Thou knowest the conduct of all in this town: how the antichrist has made his power felt; how the ministers have opposed.

Father, please, for Thy Name sake and Thy Son's sake, begin to deal with these: the scoffers and the enemies. Deal with the Baptists, my own Brotherhood . . . the Methodists and their leaders . . . .

Deal with the newspapers. O Lord, You know how the testimony of Jesus has been opposed in this city. Deal with the city councilmen and all that would try to drive us out of the city . . . .

O Dear Lord, come on Thy servant and make his messages a burning fire. Lord, give us a Pentecost here . . . . O Lord, please come to the help of Thy servant. Dear Father, make this the greatest meeting we have ever witnessed. Pour out Thy Spirit tomorrow. Dear Lord, may this city be made to tremble . . . .

O Lord, I need Your endorsement, and show this city that You are with me . . . .

In His Name . . .

The evangelist signed his name at the end of his prayer—M. F. Ham.

As He often does, the Lord answered prayer beyond all expectation. For among Mordecai Ham's converts during that 1934 Charlotte, North Carolina campaign was Frank Graham's tall, blue-eyed son—Billy.

And Edward Kimball thought he had botched the job! ❧

63

Looking for a Kind Word

One uncharacteristically awful afternoon during the 1950s, the Yankee superstar Mickey Mantle struck out three times in a row, and he was badly depressed. "When I got back to the clubhouse," he remembered, "I just sat down on my stool and held my head in my hands, like I was going to start crying. I heard someone come up to me, and it was little Tommy Berra, Yogi's boy, standing there next to me. He tapped me on the knee, nice and soft, and I figured he was going to say something nice to me, like 'You keep hanging in there' or something like that. But all he did was look at me, and then he said in his little kid's voice, 'You stink.'"*

Sometimes the only kind word you can find is the one you give yourself.

---

*Greggery C. Ward and Ken Burns, *Baseball: An Illustrated History* (New York: Alfred A. Knoph, 1994), p. 311.

64

China's First Emperor

The body of Ying Cheng, China's first emperor, was found resting in a copper coffin in a chamber sealed by a jade door, guarded by an army of six thousand colorful, life-size terracotta soldiers.

He had became a warlord at age thirteen, and for twenty-five years had battled other warlords, amassing an army of a million men and achieving dominance with brutality. He once slaughtered forty thousand soldiers in a single campaign—after they had surrendered. He devoured his enemies, it was said, "as a silkworm devours the mulberry leaf."

At the height of his power he adopted a new title: *Ch'in Shih Huang Ti*—First Divine Emperor of China. It was because of this title that we call his land China today. He boasted that he was the head of a dynasty that would last ten thousand years.

Emperor Ch'in established a strong, central monarchy, developed a uniform code of law, launched massive public works—roads and canals—and built a shining new capital. His palace alone measured a mile and a half long and a half-mile wide, with thousands of rooms and an audience hall that could seat ten thousand. It was connected via covered passageways with 270 other smaller palaces so that the Emperor could avoid assassination by sleeping in a different palace every night.

But the Emperor's most enduring monument was his Great Wall built by tens of thousands of forced laborers. According to tradition, tens of thousands of slaves died during its building, their bones being ground up and added to the mortar, making the Wall the "longest cemetery on earth." If it were in the United States, it would reach from Los Angeles to New York and back again to Chicago. At its top was a roadway wide enough for eight men marching abreast, and it was connected by twenty-five thousand towers. Signal messages could be sent across ancient China in twenty-four hours.

But Emperor Ch'in worried about dying, and he commanded his wise men, on pain of death, to find the Fountain of Youth.

They didn't.

His prime minister plotted against him, and the Divine Emperor was assassinated at age forty-one. The conspirators also forged a letter in the Emperor's name to his son and heir, bidding the son to commit suicide. He did.

Instead of enduring for ten thousand years the Emperor's dynasty was among the shortest in Chinese history.

The Emperor's murderers tried to conceal his royal body, but it rotted and began to smell, forcing them to pull a cart of salted fish nearby in an effort to obscure the odor.*

Those who appear as gods before men soon appear as men before God. Or as the 17th century British clergyman William Secker put it, "When once a man becomes a god to himself, he then becomes a devil to others."

*Adapted from *Doorways Through Time* by Stephen Bertman (Los Angeles: Jeremy P. Tarcher, Inc., 1986), chapter 20.

65

Thankfulness

We often exhibit a degree of thanksgiving in life in reverse proportion to the amount of blessings we've received. As Martin Luther wrote in his book *Table Talk:* "The greater God's gifts and works, the less they are regarded."

Among the lessons Viktor Frankl learned in the Nazi death-camp, Auschwitz, was to take time to be thankful and to count your blessings. He wrote that prisoners in the camp dreamed at night about a certain set of things more than anything else. Bread, cakes, and nice warm baths—the very things we take for granted every day.

And Frankl said that the prisoners around him began to appreciate beauty as never before. In one especially poignant paragraph, he wrote: *If someone had seen our faces on the journey from Auschwitz to a Bavarian camp as we beheld the mountains of Salzburg with their summits glowing in the sunset, through the little barred windows of our prison carriage, he would never have believed that those were the faces of men who had given up all hope of life and liberty. Despite that factor—or maybe because of it—we were carried away by nature's beauty, which we had missed for so long.*

Gerta Weissman was among the prisoners in another Nazi death camp. She recalled an episode one spring when she and her fellow inmates stood at roll call for hours on end, nearly collapsing with hunger and fatigue. But they noticed in the corner of that bleak, horrid, gray place that the concrete had broken and a flower had poked its head through. And the thousands of women there took great pains to avoid stepping on it. It was the only spot of beauty in their ugly and heinous world, and they were thankful for it.

Later in a radio interview, she added: "When people ask me, 'Why did you go on?' there is only one picture that comes to mind. The moment was when once I stood at the window of the first camp I was in and asked myself if, by some miraculous power, one wish could be granted me, what would it be? And then, with almost crystal clarity, the picture came to my mind was a picture at home—my father smoking his pipe, my mother working at her needlepoint, my brother and I doing our homework. And I remember thinking, my goodness, it was just a boring evening at home. I had known countless evenings like that. And I knew that this picture would be, if I could help it, the driving force of my survival."

Ralph Waldo Emerson observed that if the constellations appeared only once in a thousand years, imagine what an exciting event it would be. But because they're there every night, we barely give them a look.

Helen Keller once said, "I have often thought it would be a blessing if each human being were stricken blind and deaf for a few days at some time during his early adult life. It would make him more appreciative of sight and the joys of sound."

One of the evidences of the Holy Spirit's work in our lives is a gradual reversal of the twisted pattern of ingratitude. God wants to make us people who exhibit a thankfulness in proper proportion to the gifts and blessings we've received.

66

Soul Mates

Few couples have worked with greater harmony of heart and aim than Francis and Edith Schaeffer, missionaries to the intellectuals of the twentieth century. The Schaeffers set out as overseas evangelists right after World War II, and they were soon attracting hoards of university students to their chalet in the village of Huemoz in the Swiss Alps. From this came L'Abri Fellowship, founded in 1955, a study center and refuge for students and skeptics seeking answers to the great philosophical questions of life.

How the Lord brought Francis and Edith together makes a great love story. Francis grew up in Germantown in northwest Philadelphia. His parents weren't believers, and he had little exposure to Christianity. But at age seventeen, he began teaching English to a Russian immigrant, and he went to a bookstore to purchase an

English grammar book. When he returned home, he found the sales clerk had wrapped the wrong book, an introduction to Greek philosophy. As Francis studied the book, he discovered the basic philosophical questions about the meaning of life. But he found no answers until he decided to read the Bible straight through. The Scripture brought him to faith in Christ.

On Sunday night, June 26, 1932, Francis attended a service at a nearby Presbyterian church. A Unitarian came to speak on why he denied the Bible and its teachings about God, Christ, and other vital truths. A young lady in the audience had prepared herself in advance to stand and refute the man's comments. When he finished his talk, Edith gripped her notes and prepared to challenge him. Before she could rise to her feet, Francis jumped up and began shredding the speaker's arguments. Edith listened in amazement. Until that moment she had not known of anyone else in the church who believed as she did. When Francis finished, she rose and made her comments. Francis was equally impressed. After the service, he insisted on accompanying Edith home.

Thus began a lifelong partnership in taking the gospel of Jesus Christ to students and scholars in America, Europe, and among the nations.

67

More Love to Thee

All her life, Elizabeth Payson was frail and sickly, but her spirit was strong, and her ability to compose inspirational poems was striking. Her father had been one of the New England's best-loved preachers, and from him she inherited empathy and eloquence.

In 1845, at age twenty-seven, she married the pastor of Mercer Street Presbyterian Church in New York City, Dr. George L. Prentiss. She was loved by both the congregation at Mercer Street Church and the wider population in New York City. Despite physical infirmities, she cheerfully fulfilled her role as pastor's wife and mother to the couple's three beloved children.

But disaster struck in 1856 during an epidemic. Two of the couple's children died within a few weeks of the other, and for months Elizabeth was inconsolable. The members of the church did all they could, comforting the couple, bringing by food, and helping with the running of the household. But Elizabeth was devastated.

In her diary, she wrote, "Empty hands, a worn-out, exhausted body, and unutterable longings to flee from a world that has so many sharp experiences." During this time, she wrote a simple poem:

I thought that prattling boys and girls
Would fill this empty room;
That my rich heart would gather flowers
From childhood's opening bloom:
One child and two green graves are mine,
This is God's gift to me;
A bleeding, fainting, broken heart,
This is my gift to Thee.

But as Elizabeth strained to find divine comfort in her grief, the Lord directed her heart to the Old Testament story of Jacob, the man who had so many sorrows related to his children, yet God had met him in his distress and in the end it all worked for good. As she read the story from the book of Genesis, she prayed earnestly for a similar experience.

The old hymn "Nearer, My God, to Thee," occupied her thoughts, and she made it the prayer of her heart. One night, pondering these things, she composed her own poem, writing all four stanzas in one evening. Though it gave her great comfort, she didn't think her poem worthy of publication and didn't show it to anyone for thirteen years.

It has since become a classic:

More love to Thee, O Christ, More love to Thee!
Hear Thou the prayer I make On bended knee;
This is my earnest plea: More love, O Christ, to Thee,
More love to Thee, More love to Thee.

Once earthly joy I craved, sought peace and rest;
Now Thee alone I seek—Give what is best;
This all my prayer shall be: More love, O Christ, to Thee,
More love to Thee, More love to Thee.

68

Swimming for His Life

Archibald Gracie relished his swim on April 14, 1912. The ship's pool was a "six-foot tank of salt water, heated to a refreshing temperature. In no swimming bath had I ever enjoyed such pleasure before." But his account went on to say, "How near it was to being my last plunge. Before dawn of another day I would be swimming for my life in mid-ocean in a temperature of twenty-eight degrees!"

Colonel Gracie was a passenger aboard the ill-fated *Titanic*. After his swim that Sunday night aboard ship, Gracie retired to his cabin and fell asleep, only to be awakened later in the evening by "a sudden shock and noise." Dressing quickly, he ascended to the deck and learned the ship had collided with an iceberg, and he was facing almost certain death.

During the same moments in New York, his wife's sleep was also disturbed. Seized by sudden anxiety, she awoke, arose, and sank to her knees holding her prayerbook, "which by chance opened to the prayer 'For Those at Sea.'" She prayed earnestly until about 5 A.M. when the burden lifted. She rested quietly until eight when her sister "came softly to the door, newspaper in hand, to gently break the tragic news that the *Titanic* had sunk."

What had happened meantime to her husband? Colonel Gracie had done all he could to help the women and children into lifeboats, then had gone down with the ship. He later wrote: *I was in a whirlpool, swirling round and round, as I still tried to cling to the railing as the ship plunged to the depths below. Down, down, I went: it seemed a great distance. . . . Ascending back to the surface, I could see no* Titanic. *She had entirely disappeared beneath the surface of the ocean without a sign of any wave. A thin light-gray smoky vapor hung like a pall a few feet above the sea. There arose the most horrible sounds ever heard by mortal man, the agonizing cries of death from over a thousand throats. . . .*

As he bobbed in the icy waters, a new thought suddenly terrorized him. He had read of sailors being scalded to death when, in a shipwreck, the ship's boilers had exploded beneath them, turning the waters boiling hot. Swimming away from the wreckage with all his might, he congratulated himself that thus far "not one drop of sea-water was allowed to enter my mouth. With renewed determination and set jaws, I swam on."

As his strength drained away and his body began slowly freezing, Gracie nearly gave up. He prayed that somehow his spirit would comfort his wife, and he sent a message to her in his heart: "Goodbye, until we meet again in heaven." But from somewhere new strength suddenly filled Archibald Gracie's heart. As he sank below the surface, he looked up and was surprised to see the stars through the water. He pushed himself upward and collided with some of the ship's wreckage. To his left he spied an overturned lifeboat. About a dozen men had climbed on its bottom and were clinging to it as best they could.

Striking out in that direction, Gracie swam toward the boat. No one reached out a hand toward him, perhaps thinking the small craft couldn't sustain another body. But Gracie grabbed the muscular arm of one of the young men and threw his right leg across the boat, pulling himself aboard. Thus he was saved as his wife, far away in New York, knelt by her bed in earnest, effectual prayer.

Col. Archibald Gracie later wrote: *I know of no recorded instance of Providential deliverance,* he wrote, *more directly attributable to prayer.* ❧

69

The Oldest New Testament

In 1979 archaeologists in the Hinnom valley of Jerusalem discovered nine burial caves that had been carved in the rock over twenty-six hundred years ago, during the days when the descendants of David still sat on Israel's throne. Inside these tombs were two silver scrolls, rolled up and very tiny, designed to be worn on a necklace. They were caked with dirt, and so fragile that no one dared unroll them.

The Israel Museum painstakingly rinsed the scrolls in a solution of salt and acid to remove the corrosion, then sprayed them with a film-like substance. Researchers started unrolling the tiny scrolls millimeter by millimeter. Faint scratches on one of them were recognized as coming from Scripture, from Numbers 6: *The Lord bless you and keep you; the Lord make His face to shine upon you and be gracious to you. The Lord turn His face toward you and give you peace.*

The silver amulets are now known as the oldest fragment of Scripture known to man, dating back twenty-six hundred years.

When I was in college in Bristol, Tennessee, a professor in New Testament scoffed at those of us who believed that John the Apostle had actually written the Gospel of John. "It was written a couple of hundred years after John's death," said my professor. "The theology and symbolism of John is too deep to have been written so early in Christian history. Someone wrote John's Gospel later and just attached his name to it."

I later learned that my professor was strangely ignorant of archaeology.

In 1934, a little fragment, now known as the Ryland Fragment, was discovered in Egypt. Researchers found it contained verses from the eighteenth chapter of John's Gospel, and it was dated somewhere between A.D. 100–125, within scant years of John's actual composition of it.

With one small discovery, thousands of skeptical

lectures, books, articles, and dissertations were blown down like a scarecrow in a storm.

One day in 1844, a man named Constantine Tischendorf, a textual scholar, visited St. Catherine's Monastery at Mount Sinai. While there he found a basket full of old parchments to be burned, and as he examined this bundle, he recognized it as an ancient copy of Scripture. His excitement made monastery officials so suspicious they refused to cooperate with him. He spent fifteen years trying to gain that parchment, but without success. Finally he formed a friendship with the Russian Emperor. Since St. Catherine's was a Greek Orthodox Monastery, the Russian Emperor used his influence, and Tischendorf returned to St. Catherine's in hopes of retrieving the invaluable book.

But they couldn't find it. Day after day they looked until Tischendorf resigned himself to the fact that the parchments had been used for starting fires. On his last evening in the monastery, the steward mentioned to him that he had an old book. They visited the man's room, and there it was—the Bible, almost all the Old Testament and all the New Testament. Tischendorf managed to pry the parchment from the monastery as a gift for the Russian Czar.

The books remained in Russia until after the Bolshevik Revolution. On Christmas, 1933, the Communists, needing money, sold the Sinaitic Codex to England for one hundred thousand pounds. Today the Sinaitic Manuscript resides in the British Museum, virtually the entire Bible dating back to the mid-300s.

Critics charged that there had never been any Roman Governor over Palestine by the name of Pontius Pilate, as the gospel writers claimed. "The story of Christ is partly fictionalized," said the so-called scholars. "There is no record in any historical documents of anyone by that name."

But then a stone excavated in Caesarea from the first century contained the name Pontius Pilate, plainly engraved for all the world to see.

Amazingly, many scholars of the nineteenth and twentieth centuries doubted the existence of King David. Their objections centered on two things. First, the stories attributed to him are fantastic—that he was a young shepherd boy who killed a large Philistine with a slingshot and later established a royal dynasty. Second, there has never been any historical confirmation outside the Bible of a king named David.

But in 1993, a discovery among the ruins of the northern Israeli town of Dan changed that. We now have a monument from antiquity inscribed with references to the "House of David." This was the first reference to the personage of David outside the Bible, but it confirms his existence.

Someone once said that the critics keep burying the Bible, but in reality the archaeologists keep burying the critics and digging the Bible back up.

70

Shot Down

When Howard Rutledge's plane was shot down over Vietnam, he parachuted into a little village and was immediately attacked, stripped naked, and imprisoned. For the next seven years he endured brutal treatment. His food was little more than a bowl of rotting soup with a glob of pig fat—skin, hair, and all. Rats the size of cats and spiders as big as fists scurried around him. He was frequently cold, alone, and often tortured. He was sometimes shackled in excruciating positions and left for days in his own waste with carnivorous insects boring through his oozing sores. How did he keep his sanity?

In his book, *In The Presence of Mine Enemies,* Rutledge gives a powerful testimony as to the importance of Scripture memory. Some excerpts:

Now the sights and sounds and smells of death were all around me. My hunger for spiritual food soon outdid my hunger for a steak. Now I wanted to know about that part of me that will never die. Now I wanted to talk about God and Christ and the church. But in Heartbreak solitary confinement there was no pastor, no Sunday-school teacher, no Bible, no hymnbook, no community of believers to guide and sustain me. I had completely neglected the spiritual dimension of my life. It took prison to show me how empty life is without God, and so I had to go back in my memory to those Sunday School days in Tulsa, Oklahoma. If I couldn't have a Bible and hymnbook, I would try to rebuild them in my mind.

I tried desperately to recall snatches of Scripture, sermons, gospel choruses from childhood, and hymns we sang in church. The first three dozen songs were relatively easy. Every day I'd try to recall another verse or a new song. One night there was a huge thunderstorm—it was the season of the monsoon rains—and a bolt of lightning knocked out the lights and plunged the entire prison into darkness. I had been going over hymn tunes in my mind and stopped to lie down and sleep when the rains began to fall. The darkened prison echoed with wave after wave of water. Suddenly, I was humming my thirty-seventh song, one I had entirely forgotten since childhood.

Showers of blessings,
Showers of blessings we need!
Mercy drops round us are falling,
But for the showers we plead.

I no sooner had recalled those words than another song popped into my mind, the theme song of a radio program my mother listened to when I was just a kid.

Heavenly sunshine, heavenly sunshine
Flooding my soul with glory divine.
Heavenly sunshine, heavenly sunshine,
Hallelujah! Jesus is mine!

Most of my fellow prisoners were struggling like me to rediscover faith, to reconstruct workable value systems. Harry Jenkins lived in a cell nearby during much of my captivity. Often we would use those priceless seconds of communication in a day to help one another recall Scripture verses and stories.

One day I heard him whistle. When the cell block was

clear, I waited for his communication, thinking it to be some important news. "I got a new one," he said. "I don't know where it comes from or why I remember it, but it's a story about Ruth and Naomi." He then went on to tell that ancient story of Ruth following Naomi into a hostile new land and finding God's presence and protection there. Harry's urgent news was two thousand years old. It may not seem important to prison life, but we lived off that story for days, rebuilding it, thinking about what it meant, and applying God's ancient words to our predicament.

Everyone knew the Lord's Prayer and the Twenty-third Psalm, but the camp favorite verse that everyone recalled first and quoted most often is found in the Book of John, third chapter, sixteenth verse. With Harry's help I even reconstructed the seventeenth and eighteenth verses.

How I struggled to recall those Scriptures and hymns! I had spent my first eighteen years in a Southern Baptist Sunday School, and I was amazed at how much I could recall; regrettably, I had not seen then the importance of memorizing verses from the Bible, or learning gospel songs. Now, when I needed them, it was too late. I never dreamed that I would spend almost seven years (five of them in solitary confinement) in a prison in North Vietnam or that thinking about one memorized verse could have made the whole day bearable.

One portion of a verse I did remember was, "Thy word have I hid in my heart." How often I wished I had really worked to hide God's Word in my heart. I put my mind to work. Every day I planned to accomplish certain tasks. I woke early, did my physical exercises, cleaned up as best I could, then began a period of devotional prayer and meditation. I would pray, hum hymns silently, quote Scripture, and think about what the verse meant to me.

*Remember, we weren't playing games. The enemy knew that the best way to break a man's resistance was to crush his spirit in a lonely cell. In other words, some of our POWs after solitary confinement lay down in a fetal position and died. All this talk of Scripture and hymns may seem boring to some, but it was the way we conquered our enemy and overcame the power of death around us.** ❧

*Howard and Phyllis Rutledge with Mel and Lyla White, *In the Presence of Mine Enemies* (Old Tappan, NJ: Fleming H. Revell Co., 1973), excerpts taken from chapter 5.

71

Indifferentism

The world-famed Methodist missionary, E. Stanley Jones, once candidly shared how his very first sermon flopped. He recalled, "The little church was filled with my relatives and friends, all anxious that the young man should do well. I had prepared for three weeks, for I was to be God's lawyer and argue His case well. I started on a rather high key. After a half dozen sentences used a word I had never used before and I have never used since: indifferentism, whereupon a college girl smiled and put down her head.

"Her smiling so upset me that when I came back to the thread of my discourse it was gone. My mind was an absolute blank. I stood there clutching for something to say. Finally I blurted out 'I am very sorry, but I have forgotten my sermon,' and I started for my seat in shame and confusion.

"As I was about to sit down, the Inner Voice said: 'Haven't I done anything for you? If so, couldn't you tell that?' I responded to this suggestion and stepped down in front of the pulpit—I felt I didn't belong behind it—and said, 'Friends, I see I can't preach, but you know what Christ has done for my life, how He has changed me, and though I cannot preach I shall be His witness the rest of my days.'"

At the close a youth came up to me and said he wanted what I had found. It was a mystery to me then, and it is a mystery to me now that, amid my failure that night, he still saw something he wanted. As he and I knelt together, he found it. It marked a profound change in his life, and today he is a pastor, and a daughter is a missionary in Africa. As God's lawyer I was a dead failure; as God's witness I was a success. That night marked a change in my conception of the work of the Christian minister—he is to be, not God's lawyer to argue well for God; but he is to be God's witness, to tell what grace has done for an unworthy life. ❧

72

No Violence in My House

One February evening, Louise Degrafinried heard the rustling of leaves outside her secluded Tennessee home, and she cautiously peered out the window. She knew that five men had escaped from the nearby Fort Pillow State Prison, less than twenty-five miles away. They were armed and considered dangerous. "Nathan," she said to her husband, "what would we do if those men came here?"

"Honey," he replied, "we'd do just what they said."

Louise didn't like that idea at all, but she wasn't afraid. She had learned about God as a child and firmly believed her grandfather had been right in saying, "If you trust in the Lord, then He will take care of you."

Nevertheless she was glad the next morning when the sun rose. But as she was cooking breakfast and chatting with a friend on the phone, she heard Nathan shout in alarm. Louise quickly told her friend to call the police, then she hung up the phone and went to the door. There stood a tall man, covered with mud, jabbing a shotgun into Nathan's side. They stumbled into the kitchen, and the man threatened to shoot them if they didn't let him use their truck.

Nathan went outside to crank the truck as the escapee kept the shotgun trained on Louise. As soon as her husband was out the door, Louise took a few steps forward and said, "Young man!" He pointed his shotgun at her, but she seemed unafraid.

"Young man," she said again, "I'm a Christian lady. We don't have any violence in this house. This is God's house. Put down that gun." The man hesitated. "I said to put the gun down!"

Slowly he bent over and leaned the gun against the couch. Then he slumped on the couch himself and said, "Lady, I'm so hungry. I haven't eaten in three days."

"Then I will fix you breakfast," she said, cracking some more eggs into a bowl. She began talking to him, learning his name (Riley), age, and background. After saying grace over the food, she fixed a solution to help his ailing throat.

"You sound like my grandmother," said Riley, and

over breakfast he started talking sadly to Louise about his dead grandmother who had loved him.

"Well, I love you," said Louise, "and I'm not dead. Jesus loves you, too. He died for us all. That's the way I know He loves you." Riley didn't say much. He just kept eating and Louise kept giving him the Bible. Finally she said, "Young man, you'd like to give yourself up, wouldn't you?"

"Oh, lady," he replied, "They'd kill me in a minute."

"No, they won't. Not here. There won't be any violence in this house, by anyone."

Riley paused. Slowly he nodded his head. "Okay."

Within minutes, Riley was in handcuffs and headed back to prison, having gained a new prayer partner. As for Louise, she reports, "Things are pretty much back to normal now, except that I've gotten a little more attention than an old country woman should expect."*

*Adapted from Louise Degrafinried, as told to Jeffery Japinga, "The Woman Who Wasn't Afraid," in *Reader's Digest,* February, 1985, pp. 105–108, condensed from an original article in *Guideposts Magazine.*

73

The Everlasting Arms

Trinka had never been to church, and she didn't want to go now. She planted her feet in the gravel, defying our efforts to lure her toward the car. We coaxed and cajoled; we baited and waited; we bribed and threatened. We even tied a rope around her neck and tried to drag her.

We wanted to take her because our church had planned a city-wide celebration that included a small petting zoo. Our daughter, Hannah, had promised to bring Trinka, her pet sheep. We had purchased Trinka as a lamb, bottle-feeding her until she was old enough for grain and grass. Now she was fat, fleecy and heavy. But Trinka hated the station wagon and refused to go near its open tailgate.

I edged near her, stooped down, and spoke to her. Then I slid my arms under her woolly belly, and both of us grunted as I lifted her from the ground, cradled her to my chest, and carried her to the car.

Halfway to the car I suddenly thought of Deuteronomy 33:27: "The eternal God is your refuge, and underneath are the everlasting arms."

I had read that verse many times. I had visualized it as a pair of cupped hands holding people. But Moses, the writer of Deuteronomy, said, "Underneath are the everlasting *arms,*" not the "everlasting *hands.*"

As a child, I had also pictured this verse along the lines suggested by the hymn "Leaning on the Everlasting Arms." I imagined a staggering soul supported by a friend's stalwart arms around his waist. But the verse doesn't say *around* us. It says *underneath* us.

Now it made sense. Before delivering Israel from the clutches of Pharaoh, Moses had tended Jethro's flock for forty years in the deserts of Arabia. He had carried hundreds of sheep over difficult terrain, away from dangerous ravines and imminent danger. He had scooped up many an injured lamb.

Furthermore, Moses was speaking to a nation of shepherds. God had told Moses and Aaron, "Your children will be shepherds here for forty years." So when Moses spoke of God's arms beneath them, the people of Israel must have remembered the many times that their own arms had slid beneath the fuzzy undersides of ewes and rams and lambs. They understood.

Now so did I. The bleeding Savior died for bleating sheep. And He rose again, for the Good Shepherd is the eternal God. When I face my own "terrifying tailgates," why do I struggle? Those everlasting arms support me when I face harms or alarms. The Lord God hugs me from beneath and loves me from above. I have a grip on life, because He has a grip on me.

The prophet Isaiah understood this picture. He wrote, "He tends His flock like a shepherd: He gathers the lambs in His arms and carries them close to His heart."

But are the everlasting arms just for little lambs? No, for later in the book of Isaiah God said, "Even to your old age and gray hairs I . . . will sustain you. I have made you, and I will carry you."

Trinka seemed to have a great time that afternoon at the celebration. The tailgate that she so feared brought her to the children whom she enjoyed. Later that evening as I lifted her from the car and returned her to her own pasture, I thought, "What more could a sheep need than green pastures, still waters—and loving arms?"

74

The Art of Forgiving Yourself

In his book, *Healing for Damaged Emotions,* David Seamands writes about a young minister who once came to see him. He was having a lot of problems getting along with other people, especially his wife and family.

Seamands recalls: "I had already talked privately with his wife; she was a fine person—attractive, warm, affectionate, loving—and totally supported him in his ministry. But he was continually criticizing her, scapegoating her. Everything she did was wrong. He was sarcastic and demanding, and withdrew from her advances, rejecting her love and affection. Slowly but surely it began to dawn on him: he was destroying their marriage.

"Then he realized that in his weekend pastorate

he was hurting people through sermons which were excessively harsh and judgmental . . . .

"Finally, in his desperation, he came to see me. At the beginning of our interview, he met trouble like a real man: he blamed it on his wife! But after a while, when he became honest, the painful root of the matter came to light."

The young minister finally admitted that while serving in the armed forces in Korea, he had spent two weeks of rest and relaxation in Japan. During that leave, walking the streets of Tokyo, feeling empty, lonely, and terribly homesick, he fell into temptation and went three or four times to a prostitute.

He had never been able to forgive himself. He had sought God's forgiveness and, with his head, believed he had it. But the guilt still plagued him and he hated himself. Every time he looked in the mirror, he couldn't stand what he was seeing. He had never shared this with anyone, and the burden was becoming intolerable.

When he returned home to marry his fiancée, who had faithfully waited for him all those years, his emotional conflicts increased because he still could not accept complete forgiveness. He couldn't forgive himself for what he had done to himself and to her; so he couldn't accept her freely offered affection and love. He felt he had no right to be happy. His sense of guilt slowly poisoned his personality, his emotions, and his relationships with other people.

"How beautiful it was to see him receive full, free forgiveness from God," Seamands wrote, "then from his wife, and perhaps best of all, from himself."

The hands of the Apostle Paul had once held the documents that sent Christians to prison, ripping apart families, tearing up churches. His hands had even once held the garments of those who stoned the church's first martyr, the godly young man Stephen. How did he get over the guilt and shame? He said in 1 Corinthians 15:9–11:

For I am the least of the apostles, who am not worthy to be called an apostle, because I persecuted the church of God. But by the grace of God I am what I am, and His grace toward me was not in vain; but I labored more abundantly than they all, yet not I, but the grace of God which was with me.

Paul, having been forgiven by God, chose to forgive himself, and he devoted the rest of his life to preaching the gospel he had once labored to destroy. He spent his days seeking to strengthen what he had once sought to tear down. He considered himself a debtor. While he could never make up for his sin or atone for his guilt, he could dedicate himself to help those whom he had previously hurt and extend the church he had once opposed.

His forgiveness fueled his Christian service.

What can wash away my sin?
Nothing—but the blood of Jesus.

75

Come Thou Fount of Every Blessing

The seventeen-year-old grinned mischievously as he poured another drink for the fortune-teller. He and his buddies, relaxed by their alcohol, laughed as the gypsy tried to tell their futures through her drunken haze. But he stopped laughing when she pointed a quivering finger at him and said, "And you, young man, you will live to see your children and grandchildren."

Something about those words bothered young Robert Robinson, and his mood changed. "Let's go," he told his friends, "She's too drunk to know what she's saying. Leave her alone."

But her words bothered Robert, for he thought, "If

I'm going to live to see my children and grandchildren, I'll have to change my ways. I can't keep on like I'm going now."

That evening, Robert suddenly suggested to his buddies they attend the evangelistic meeting being held by world-famous George Whitefield. "Sure," they said, "maybe we can break up the meeting."

But that evening Whitefield, preaching from Matthew 3:7, thundered out the words "O generation of vipers! Flee from the wrath to come!" At one point during his sermon, Whitefield paused, tried to control himself, then burst into tears, exclaiming, "Oh, my hearers! The wrath to come! The wrath to come!"

The effects of Robert's day-long drinking disappeared, and he sobered up immediately. He felt Whitefield was preaching directly to him, and the words haunted him for two years and seven months until, on December 10, 1755, Robinson, age twenty, gave his heart to Christ.

Robert Robinson joined the Methodists and was appointed by John Wesley to minister in Norfolk, England. He later became a Baptist and for the rest of his life pastored a small church in Cambridge, England, known as the Congregation of Stone Yard. Those who heard him were impressed with his forceful preaching, and in 1790, Robert, age fifty-four, was invited to deliver a sermon at the Birmingham pulpit of the well-known minister, Dr. Priestly.

The following morning, June 9, 1790, his host came to Robert's room and knocked on the door. There was no answer. Robert had died peacefully during the night in his sleep.

Years before, not long after he had begun preaching, Robert Robinson had written a few verses with which to conclude his sermon, and it is these words for which he is most remembered to this day. It has been a favorite hymn of the church for over two centuries:

Come, Thou Fount of every blessing,
Tune my heart to sing Thy grace;
Streams of mercy, never ceasing,
Call for songs of loudest praise:
Teach me some melodious sonnet,
Sung by flaming tongues above;
Praise the mount—I'm fixed upon it—
Mount of Thy redeeming love.

Take a moment and pray or sing this prayer as your own. And remember the strange story of its author. God can do a great deal with incorrigible seventeen-year-old boys when He gets hold of them. He knows how to "tune our hearts to sing his grace." ❧

Through the Bible

Geoffery Bull, British missionary to Tibet, was captured and imprisoned by Chinese Communists who took Bull's possessions from him, threw him in a series of prisons, and even robbed him of his Bible. His captors seemed determined to make the missionary suffer, and for three years he faced extreme temperatures, miserable physical conditions, bodily abuse, and near starvation. Bull was subjected to such mental and psychological torture that he feared he would go insane.

How did he keep his mind at peace? He had no Bible now, but he had studied the Bible all his life. So he began to systematically go over the Scriptures in his mind. He found it took him about six months to go all the way through the Bible mentally. Lying on his mat, he would start at Genesis, and would recall each incident and story as best he could, first concentrating on the content and then musing on certain points, seeking light in prayer.

He continued through the Old Testament, reconstructing the books and chapters as best he could, then into the New Testament and on to Revelation. Then he started over again.

He later wrote, "The strength received through this meditation was, I believe, a vital factor in bringing me through, kept by the faith to the very end." ❧

77

To Hell and Back

Dr. Maurice Rawlings, M.D., cardiologist and professor of medicine at the University of Tennessee College of Medicine in Chattanooga, was a devout atheist who considered all religion "hocus-pocus." To him, death was nothing more than a painless extinction.

But in 1977, Rawlings was resuscitating a man who came back from the edge of death. The man was terrified and screaming. Rawlings wrote: *Each time he regained heartbeat and respiration, the patient screamed, "I am in hell!" He was terrified and pleaded with me to help him. I was scared to death . . . . Then I noticed a genuinely alarmed look on his face. He had a terrified look worse than the expression seen in death! This patient had a grotesque grimace expressing sheer horror! His pupils were dilated, and he was perspiring and trembling—he looked as if his hair was on end.*

Dr. Rawlings, shaken, became intrigued with near death experiences, and as he researched the subject, doing much of his study first-hand, he discovered something that has been omitted by much of the prevailing literature. There are many stories of near-death experiences in which people report moving down a peaceful tunnel toward a gentle light, but Dr. Rawlings' research, which later appeared in *Omni* Magazine, demonstrated that about fifty percent near-death victims report seeing lakes of fire, devil-like figures and other sights reflecting the darkness of hell.

"Just listening to these patients has changed my whole life," claims Dr. Rawlings. "There is a life after death, and if I don't know where I'm going, it's not safe to die."

Through these experiences, Dr. Rawlings began studying what the Bible had to say about hell and other subjects, and he became a Christian.*

The realities of heaven and hell are closer than we think, and the Bible minces no words: "Prepare to meet

*For fascinating reading, check Dr. Rawling's two books on this subject: *Beyond Death's Door* (Bantam, 1979) and *To Hell and Back* (Thomas Nelson, 1996).

your God" (Amos 4:12). But Jesus—God made flesh—died and rose from the grave to rob death of its sting and to deny hell its victims. "This," he said in John 17:3, "is eternal life, that they may know You, the only true God, and Jesus Christ whom You have sent."

78

The Fulton Street Revival

God often sends revival when times are worst. The mood of America was grim during the mid-1850s. The country was teetering on the brink of civil war, torn by angry voices and impassioned opinions. A depression had halted railroad construction and factory output. Banks were failing, unemployment soared. Spiritual lethargy permeated the land.

In New York City, Jeremiah C. Lanphier, a layman, accepted the call of the North Reformed Dutch Church to begin a full-time program of evangelism. He visited door-to-door, placed posters in boarding houses, and prayed. But the work languished and Lanphier grew discouraged.

As autumn fell over the city, Lanphier decided to try noontime prayer meetings, thinking that businessmen might attend during their lunch hours. He announced the first one for September 23, 1857, at the Old Dutch Church on Fulton Street. When the hour came, Lanphier found himself alone. He sat and waited. Finally, one man showed up, then a few others.

But the next week, twenty came. The third week, forty. Someone suggested the meetings occur daily, and within months the building was overflowing. Other churches opened their doors. The revival spread to other cities. Offices and stores closed for prayer at noon. Newspapers spread the story, even telegraph companies set aside certain hours during which businessmen could wire one another with news of the revival.

In all these cities, the same routine was followed. Prayer services began at noon and ended at one. People could come and go as they pleased. The service opened with a hymn, followed by the sharing of testimonies and prayer requests. A time limit of five minutes per speaker was enforced by a small bell which jingled when anyone exceeded the limit. Virtually no great preachers or famous Christians were used. It was primarily a lay movement, led by the gentle moving of God's Spirit.

The Fulton Street Revival—sometimes called "The Third Great Awakening"—lasted nearly two years, and between five hundred thousand and one million people were said to have been converted. Out of it came the largest outlay of money for philanthropic and Christian causes America had yet experienced.

How long has it been since you last prayed for another revival? Why not memorize this verse and present it to the Lord with persistence until He answers:

Will You not revive us again, that Your people may rejoice in You?—Psalm 85:6

79

Bat Out of Hell

Mitsuo Fuchida, commander of the Japanese Air Force, led the squadron of 860 planes that attacked Pearl Harbor on December 7, 1941.

American bomber Jacob DeShazer was eager to strike back, and the following April 18th, he flew his B-25 Bomber, the "Bat Out of Hell," on a dangerous raid over Japan. After dropping his bombs on Nagoya, DeShazer lost his way in heavy fog and ejected as his plane ran out of fuel. He was taken prisoner, tortured by the Japanese, and threatened with imminent death. For almost two years, DeShazer suffered hunger, cold, and dysentery. He hated his captors and treated the guards with contempt.

In May of 1944, he was given a Bible. "You can keep it for three weeks," said the guard. DeShazer grabbed it, clutched it to his chest, and started reading in Genesis. Scarcely sleeping, he read the Bible through several times, memorizing key passages. On June 8, coming to Romans 10:9, Jacob prayed to receive Jesus Christ as his Savior.

Immediately Matthew 5:44 became a critical text for DeShazer: *But I say to you, love your enemies, bless those who curse you, do good to those who hate you, and pray for those who spitefully use you and persecute you.*

DeShazer determined with God's help to treat his Japanese guards differently. His hostility toward them evaporated, and every morning he greeted them warmly. He prayed for them and sought to witness to them. He noticed their attitude toward him also changed, and they would often slip him food or supplies.

After the war, DeShazer returned to Japan as a missionary. Copies of his testimony, "I Was a Prisoner of the Japanese," flooded the country, and thousands wanted to see the man who could love and forgive his enemies. DeShazer settled down to establish a church in Nagoya, the city he had bombed. One man in particular, deeply affected by DeShazer's testimony, was led to Christ by Glenn Wagner of the Pocket Testament League. Shortly afterward, the man paid a visit to Jacob DeShazer at his home, and the two became dear friends and brothers. It was Mitsuo Fuchida, who had led the Pearl Harbor attack. As DeShazer served as missionary in Japan, Fuchida became a powerful national evangelist, preaching the gospel throughout Japan and around the world.

Jesus often sends us to former enemies in order to demonstrate the extent of His love and the breadth of his forgiveness. Think of a person who seems unlikely to ever be your friend—or the Lord's. That may just be the one God wants you to reach. He has his ways.

80

John Hooper

During the reign of England's Mary I—Bloody Mary—Rev. John Hooper was imprisoned for his faith and sentenced to die for preaching the gospel. About nine o'clock on the morning of February 9, 1555, he was taken to the center of Gloucester. About seven thousand people were present, it being market day. Hooper nodded cheerfully to friends; then arriving at the stake, he removed his outer clothes while sacks of gunpowder were tied to his armpits and between his legs.

As the silent crowd gazed in terror, Hooper raised his voice and asked them to join him in the Lord's Prayer. The winter sky echoed with seven thousand voices: "Our Father which art in heaven, Hallowed be Thy name. Thy kingdom come. Thy will be done in earth, as it is in heaven. . . ."

The final "Amen" was spoken, and the multitudes watched through tear-clouded eyes as a metal hoop was placed around Hooper's chest to hold him to the stake. The fire was set, but too much green wood had been used, and the wind was strong. It created a slow torture, with Hooper's hair burning a little and his skin swelling from the heat, but without any lethal flames.

Finally the lower part of his body began to smoke as the executioners got a blaze going. Even when his face and mouth blackened, he could be seen praying until his lips finally burned away. John Foxe wrote in his Book of Martyrs: *Hooper struck at his chest until one of his arms fell off, and then continued striking his chest with the other hand while fat, water, and blood spurted out his fingertips. Hooper was about forty-five minutes to an hour in the fire. Even so he was like a lamb. Now he reigns as a blessed martyr in the joys of heaven prepared for the faithful in Christ before the foundations of the world.**

In our pleasure-driven world, we may forget that some stories are not meant to entertain, but to edify. This story isn't fun to read, but I always come away from it holding my faith more seriously and my possessions more lightly. ❧

*John Fox, *The New Foxes Book of Martyrs,* written and updated by Harold J. Chadwick (New Brunswick, NJ: Bridge-Logos Publishers, 1997), p. 177.

81

New Beginnings

My first counseling session was a hoot! I was a newly-installed pastor, young, ill-equipped and green as grass. A troubled young couple came to my office for counseling, not knowing they were my first guinea pigs. From the moment they sat down, they snarled at each other like cats. They seemed particularly in a stew over the raising of their two-year-old child. I tried to offer some words of wisdom, but nothing in my schooling had prepared me to referee a mud-wrestling match. They grew angrier and louder by the moment.

I finally lost temper with them. "That's it!" I shouted, banging my fist on the table. "You're as immature as your toddler, and I don't think anyone can help you, least of all me." I rose and walked to the door. "I can't even get a word in edgewise. Good-bye."

Stunned by my tirade, they cautiously rose and

edged out of the door. They were halfway to their car when I shouted behind them, "And I'll tell you another thing. In 14 years, your son's going to be here in my office, needing counseling for the mess you're making of him!" I slammed the door for good measure.

That was the last I saw of them for a year. Then one day the husband walked into my office. "You know," he told me, "I want to thank you for what you said to us. We were so shocked we decided to begin rebuilding our home from scratch. You wouldn't believe what a difference it's made."

I later considered all this. I had badly botched the initial counseling job, but God, in His mercy, reclaimed it. In the process, he taught a struggling, young couple one of His greatest lessons: the privilege of new beginnings. Proverbs 24:16 says, "No matter how often an honest man falls, he always gets up again . . ." (TEV).

The first person to invent the wheel only discovered what God had already designed, for the Lord created things in circles. The stars and planets are round, they move in orbital circuits, and life, as a result, moves in cycles. Every 365 days, we have a new year; every 24 hours, we have a new day; every 60 minutes we have a new hour. God created the potential for new beginnings into the very design of the universe.

No matter how bad things seem, there's always hope.

There is always room for a new beginning. ❧

82

And Me Carrying a Grudge!

The great Methodist pastor Charles Allen wrote that when he was in the fourth grade, the superintendent of the school mistreated him. There was no doubt about it. It was a deliberate wrong which the man committed because he had fallen out with Charles' father.

The Allens moved from that town, and the years passed.

One day during Charles' first pastorate, he heard that his old antagonist was seeking a job with the schools in the area. Charles knew that as soon as he told his friends on the school board about the man, they would not hire him.

I went out to get in my car to go see some of the board members, and suddenly it came over me what I had done.

Here I was out trying to represent Him who was nailed to the cross, and me carrying a grudge! That realization was a humiliating experience. I went back into my house, knelt by my bedside, and said, "Lord, if you will forgive me of this, I will never be guilty of it anymore." That experience and that promise are among the best things that ever happened in my life.

83

God Will Take Care of You

James Cash Penney, coming from a long line of Baptist preachers, grew up with deep convictions. He was unwaveringly honest. He never smoked or drank, and he was a hard worker. But in 1929 when the Great Depression hit, Penney found himself in crisis. He had made unwise commitments, and they turned sour. Penney began to worry about them, and soon he was unable to sleep. He developed a painful case of shingles and was hospitalized. His anxiety only increased in the hospital, and it seemed resistant to tranquilizers and drugs. His mental state deteriorated until, as he later said, *I was broken nervously and physically, filled with despair, unable to see even a ray of hope. I had nothing to live for. I felt I hadn't a friend left in the world, that even my family turned against me.*

One night he was so oppressed he didn't think his

heart would hold out, and, expecting to die before morning, he sat down and wrote farewell letters to his wife and sons.

But he did live through the night, and the next morning he heard singing coming from the little hospital chapel. The words of the song said,

Be not dismayed whate'er betide
God will take care of you.

Entering the chapel, he listened to the song, to the Scripture reading, and to the prayer. *Suddenly—something happened. I can't explain it. I can only call it a miracle. I felt as if I had been instantly lifted out of the darkness of a dungeon into warm, brilliant sunlight.*

All worry left him as he realized more fully than he had ever imagined just how much the Lord Jesus Christ cared for him. From that day J. C. Penney was never plagued with worry, and he later called those moments in the chapel "the most dramatic and glorious twenty minutes of my life."

When he died at age ninety-five, he left behind 1,660 department stores in his name and a legacy of integrity that honors Christ to this day.

84

Ingenious Evangelists

The growth of the Korean Church is among the greatest legacies of modern Christianity. Some of the largest churches on earth are in South Korea. But the growth of the gospel there came at a cost.

How *did* Christianity first come to this part of the world? The first Catholic missionaries arrived in the 1700s and were badly persecuted. The first Protestant missionary, Carl Gutzlaff, stayed only a month in 1832. The next, Robert Thomas, arrived in 1876 to become the first Protestant martyr there. Finally, on July 11, 1886, missionary Horace Underwood secretly administered the first Protestant baptism on Korean soil to a Mr. Toh Sa No.

But was Mr. No really the first convert?

In his book *What in the World is God Doing?* Dr. Ted Engstrom relates a story told him by a veteran Korean

Christian. In the early 1880s, three Korean workmen, laboring in China, heard the gospel and embraced the Lord Jesus. The three soon conspired about getting the message of Christ into their own country, an action forbidden by the government. Since the Korean and Chinese alphabets were similar, they decided to smuggle in a copy of the Chinese Bible. They drew straws to see who would have the privilege of bringing the gospel into Korea.

The first man buried the Bible in his belongings and headed toward the border, a journey of many days by footpath. There he was searched, found out, and killed. Word reached the others that their friend was dead. The second man tore pages from his Bible and hid the separate pages throughout his luggage. He, too, made the long trip to the border only to be searched and beheaded.

The third man grew more determined than ever to succeed. He ingeniously tore his Bible apart page by page, folding each page into a tiny strip. He wove the strips into a rope and wrapped his baggage in his homemade rope. When he came to the border, the guards asked him to unwrap his belongings. Finding nothing amiss, they admitted him.

The man arrived home, untied the rope, and ironed out each page. He reassembled his Bible and began to preach Christ wherever he went. And when the missionaries of the 1880s fanned into the country, they found the seed already sown and the firstfruits appearing.

85

The Gambler

Gambling can take a man's shirt off his back, but Christ can clothe him with hope. Camillus de Lellis learned both lessons. He was an Italian, born in 1550 to a mother nearly sixty. By age seventeen, he stood six-and-a-half feet, big boned, well muscled, quick tempered, and unchaste. He enlisted in the army, was sent to war, but on the battlefield contracted a leg disease that afflicted him the rest of his life.

The hospital for incurables in Rome, San Giacomo, admitted him, but he was soon ejected for quarreling. That wasn't his worst fault. Camillus relished betting, and by 1574 his addiction had taken his last penny. That autumn in the streets of Naples he gambled with his last possession, the shirt on his back. Losing the wager, he stripped it off and limped away both broke and broken.

Camillus secured a construction job, and one day a

friar came along preaching. The message hit home, and Camillus fell to his knees, crying to God for mercy. He was twenty-five years old when he became a Christian. He returned to San Giacomo and offered himself a volunteer. He ministered intently to the suffering, and in time he was promoted. Then promoted again. He eventually became hospital superintendent.

With a friend's endowment, he organized a small army of male nurses to serve the sick in Christ's name. He also mobilized volunteers to travel with troops in Hungary and Croatia, thus forming the first "military field ambulance." He sent nurses aboard galley ships to attend slaves suffering from pestilence. In all, Camillus organized eight hospitals, pioneered medical hygiene and diet, and successfully opposed the prevailing practice of burying patients alive.

All the while, Camillus' leg was worsening, and he began suffering ruptures elsewhere on his body. Sometimes on his rounds, he crawled from sickbed to sickbed. On July 14, 1614, after a final tour of his works, Camillus de Lellis died at age sixty-four. He was canonized in 1746 and declared patron saint of the sick by Pope Leo XIII and of nurses and nursing by Pope Pius XI. In

Catholic tradition he is remembered every year on July 14th.

Gambling, in its many forms, can momentarily entertain, superficially enrich, and permanently impoverish. God, with His wondrous grace, can abundantly forgive, permanently transform, and eternally deliver. Which seems to be the safest bet to you? ❧

86

Unclogging the Pipeline

Victor Guaminga, an Ecuadorian Christian, is a World Vision project coordinator in his own country. Wanting to eradicate water-borne diseases in his home village, Laime Chico, Victor developed a plan for building a pipeline to supply the villagers with clean, drinkable water from a source some distance away.

Unfortunately, the best path for such a pipeline was right through Laime San Carlos, a rival village—one with which Victor's village had a long-lasting feud.

When certain implacable enemies in the rival village heard about the proposed water line, they made it known that they would destroy any pipes laid for that purpose. Therefore the whole plan was stymied.

In spite of their neighbors' hostility, however, Christians in Victor's village, knowing that the other village had no church, decided to conduct an evangelistic effort there.

Doing so was both difficult and dangerous. Not many of the rival village's people paid any attention to the evangelizers. But four did respond to the gospel message and became believers in Christ.

After being spiritually nurtured by believers from Victor's church, the four converts became faithful witnesses to others in their own village. Slowly, a church formed there also.

Eventually the very man who had most vehemently opposed the water project became a believer himself. Seeing, then, how wrong his attitude had been, he asked forgiveness and gave his cooperation to the project.

Five years after that project in Ecuador was proposed, clean, drinkable water flowed through dependable pipes not only to Victor's village but to the formerly hostile one, plus two other nearby villages. And now there are growing churches in all four places.*

Ever notice how things tend to work for good whenever we hear God's divine "advice," like:

*Adapted from "Example in Ecuador: Forgiveness Unclogs a Pipeline," in World Vision, February-March, 1986, p. 18.

A soft answer turns away wrath.—Proverbs 15:1

If it is possible, as much as depends on you, live peaceably with all men.—Romans 12:18

Do all things without complaining and disputing, that you may become blameless and harmless, children of God without fault in the midst of a crooked and perverse generation, among whom you shine as lights in the world, holding fast to the word of life.—Philippians 2:14–16 ❧

87

Curse Ye Woodchuck

The Puritans of Colonial New England appointed "tithingmen" to stroll among the pews on Sunday mornings, alert for anyone nodding off during the long, sometimes ponderous sermons. They carried long poles with feathers on one end and knobs or sharp thorns on the other. Worshippers napped at their own peril, and the results were unpredictable—as noted by Obadiah Turner of Lynn, Massachusetts, in his journal for June 3, 1646:

Allen Bridges hath bin chose to wake ye sleepers in meeting. And being much proude of his place, must needs have a fox taile fixed to ye ende of a long staff wherewith he may brush ye faces of them yt will have napps in time of discourse, likewise a sharpe thorne whereby he may pricke such as be most sound. On ye last Lord his day, as hee strutted about ye meetinghouse, he did spy Mr. Tomlins sleeping with much comfort, hys head kept steadie by being in ye corner, and his hand grasping ye rail. And soe spying, Allen did quickly thrust his staff behind Dame Ballard and give him a grievous prick upon ye hand. Whereupon Mr. Tomlins did spring vpp mch above ye floore, and with terrible force strike hys hand against ye wall; and also, to ye great wonder of all, prophanlie exclaim in a loud voice, curse ye wood-chuck, he dreaming so it seemed yt a wood-chuck had seized and bit his hand. But on coming to know where he was, and ye greate scandall he had committed, he seemed much abashed, but did not speak. And I think he will not soon again goe to sleepe in meeting."

88

That's Our Tithe!

Lyle Eggleston served as a missionary for many years in a little town on the rocky coast of northern Chile. In time, the congregation grew to about eighty adults, but Eggleston was concerned that the Christians in that area didn't seem able to support their own national pastor. The people were very poor, and the church's offerings amounted to no more than six dollars a month.

One day, Eggleston brought the problem to the Lord during a definite time of prayer. A few weeks later he stopped to visit a middle-aged couple, new converts who had begun the habit of reading their Bibles every day.

"What does the word tithing mean?" asked Manuel. "We ran into that in our reading, and we don't understand it."

Eggleston didn't really want to answer the question, for he knew that Manuel and his wife were unemployed and on the verge of destitution. They were somehow managing to feed themselves and their twenty-five Rhode Island hens on the income from the eggs laid each day.

Nevertheless they insisted he explain the concept of tithing to them, so he turned to 1 Corinthians 16 and 2 Corinthians 8 and 9 where Paul urged believers to lay aside each week a portion of their income to the Lord.

The following Sunday Manuel handed Lyle an envelope and, smiling, said, "That's our tithe!" Inside were a few bills amounting to about nineteen cents.

The next Sunday afternoon, the couple flagged down Lyle as he rode his bicycle past their house. They had some exciting news. The Tuesday morning after they had given their tithe, there wasn't a bite for breakfast nor any money. Their first impulse was to take the few pesos that had accumulated in their "tithe box," but on second thought they said, "No. That's God's money. We will go without breakfast this morning."

There was nothing to do but tend the hens. Much to their surprise, there were eggs in the nests that had usually at that hour been empty. Later in the day, a little man came along with a pushcart wanting fertilizer. They cleaned out their hen house, and the manure brought a good price. After buying groceries, there was enough money left over for the wife to purchase a pair of shoes, so she rode the bus twelve kilometers around the bay into a larger town. There she bumped into a nephew she had not seen in five years, and who, to her utter surprise, owned a shoe store. After she had found just the pair she wanted, he wrapped them for her and handed her the package with these words, "Oh no, Aunt, I can't take your money. These shoes are a gift from me."

The following week, Manuel got a job on a project that would last for two years, and soon the little couple was tithing on a much larger salary. Word got around the church, and others began experimenting with giving. Soon the church's income begin to rise dramatically, and they were able to pay their own rent and utility bills, support a national pastor who was working with Indians, and, in a short time, they were able to call and finance a pastor of their own.

Lyle Eggleston and his wife were able to move to a new location and start a new work as the little church grew in numbers, size, property, and faith. "We had offered up a bit of prayer and nineteen cents," Lyle later said, "and God did the rest."*

*Lyle Eggleston, "The Church That Learned to Give," in *Moody Magazine,* July/August, 1988, pp. 31–32.

89

Save the Children

One morning years ago, I took a walking tour of Albany, New York, stopping for lunch on a park bench. As I ate my sandwich, I felt someone staring at me. Turning around, I saw a little fellow watching me with intense interest. He appeared to be eleven or twelve, his eyes were big, and his face crinkled with curiosity.

"What's your name?" he finally asked. Then, "What you eatin'? Where you from? Tennessee? Where's that? What're you doin' here?" To the last question, I told him I had come to Albany to preach at a church.

"What does it mean to preach?" he asked.

"It means to tell others about Jesus," I replied. When I said the word "Jesus," his eyes widened, and he cupped his hand over his mouth.

"Jesus," he whispered, "Mister, don't you know?"

"Know what?"

"That's a cuss word."

It dawned on me that the only time this boy had ever heard the name *Jesus* was as a profanity in his home and in his neighborhood haunts.

Compare that little fellow's history with the Apostle Paul's description of Timothy's upbringing: *From childhood (from infancy—*NIV*), you have known the Holy Scriptures, which are able to make you wise for salvation through faith which is in Jesus Christ (2 Timothy 3:15).*

Children can surely come to know the Lord Jesus Christ. Polycarp, the great church father, was nine when he was saved. Matthew Henry was eleven. Jonathan Edwards, America's greatest theologian, was seven. Hymnwritter Isaac Watts was nine. Evangelist Henry Drummond, Moody's friend, was nine.

E. Stanley Jones, the great Methodist missionary statesman, was moved to be a missionary when he was eight years old. He saw a picture of a big tiger standing beside a small Indian boy, and underneath was the caption, "Who will tell me about Jesus?" And Stanley Jones said, "I will."

Corrie ten Boom asked Christ to be her Savior at

age five. W. A. Criswell, the famous Southern Baptist pastor, was saved when he was ten, but he felt God calling him into ministry even earlier. "I had been thinking about being a preacher for years, since I was six," he recalled. "I knew I wasn't converted yet, hadn't been saved. But I knew God wanted me to be a preacher."

Hymnist Philip Bliss was twelve years old when he made his public confession of Christ. William Booth, founder of the Salvation Army, was fifteen. Dr. Harry Ironside was thirteen. Count Nickolaus Ludwig Zinzendorf, who gave rise to modern Protestant missions, was saved at age four.

Returning to his friend's home after conducting meetings in a town in England, D. L. Moody was asked by his host, "How many were converted tonight in the meeting?"

"Two and a half," replied Moody.

"What do you mean?" asked his friend. "Were there two adults and a child?"

"No," said the evangelist, "it was two children and an adult. The children have given their lives to Christ in their youth, while the adult has come with half of his life."

90

White Christmas?

Without Jesus to wash us whiter than snow, there can never be a genuinely *white* Christmas.

Consider Lindsay, for example. His father, a distant and severe man, drove him especially hard during the holidays. Lindsay was given extra chores at the family ranch, and his old man whipped him if he didn't work hard enough. Lindsay lived in fear of these beatings, which often drew blood. But even worse were the verbal floggings, the names, the insults, the belittling put-downs. They seemed especially harsh at Christmas.

The memories stayed with him all his life, tormenting him like demons every December. One friend said, "Lindsay was never able to find happiness. He became a hard-drinking hell-raiser who went from woman to woman and couldn't find peace or success."

Finally at age fifty-one, he angrily watched Bing

Crosby's "White Christmas" one last time on television, then put a gun to his head and a bullet through his brain.

"I hated Christmas because of Pop, and I always will," he once said. "It brings back the pain and fear I suffered as a child. And if I ever do myself in, it will be at Christmastime. That will show the world what I think of Bing Crosby's White Christmas."

Ironically, sadly, he was Bing's son—Lindsay Crosby.

That bizarre story is itself a parable of what happens when we gut Christmas of its true glory. If only Lindsay had really understood that Jesus Christ was born on Christmas day so that our sins, though they be as scarlet, shall be as white as snow. Though they are red like crimson, they shall be as wool (Isaiah 1:18).

91

Discouragement in the Ministry

"No, I do not become discouraged," Mother Teresa once said, in answer to a question. "You see, God has not called me to a ministry of success. He has called me to a ministry of mercy."

William Carey, the "Father of Modern Missions" labored for seven years in India before baptizing his first convert. Mary Drewery, in her biography of Carey, said, "The number of actual conversions directly attributable to him is pathetically small; the number indirectly attributable to him must be legion."

America's first missionary, Adoniram Judson, labored for seven years in Burma before seeing his first convert.

Robert Morrison, the founder of Protestant missions in China, labored for seven years before his first convert was won to Christ.

On May 16, 1819, Pomare II was baptized—the first convert on the island of Tahiti after twenty-two years of tears and toil by missionaries Mr. and Mrs. Henry Nott.

Missionary Allen Gardiner traveled repeatedly to South America, trying to evangelize the islands of Patagonia and Tierra del Fuego. He eventually died of starvation without seeing a single soul saved, but the South American Missionary Society he founded has been sending missionaries and saving souls for over one hundred and fifty years.

Jimmy Aldridge and his colleagues with Free Will Baptist Foreign Missions worked for nine years in Bondoukou in the Ivory Coast of West Africa before seeing their first converts in the villages.

In 1939 the first Sudan Interior Mission workers went to Doro in southern Sudan to share the gospel with the Mabaan people, who had never heard of Christ. Years passed, and three SIM workers were buried at Doro and more than fifty worked there diligently from 1939 to 1964 when they had to leave because of civil war. When they left, there were few baptized believers in good standing. But when they later returned to the Sudan, they were amazed to find large groups of witnessing believers with nearly three hundred waiting to be baptized.

W. A. Criswell was perhaps the best-known pastor in the world during his long tenure at the First Baptist Church of Dallas, Texas. His sermons, personal efforts, and multiplied books have been the means of winning untold numbers to Christ.

But in Criswell's biography, author Billy Keith tells an interesting story about the man who led Criswell to the Lord. It was when W. A. was ten years old, and Rev. John Hicks came to his small Texas town to conduct a revival meeting. Hicks stayed in the Criswell home during his two week campaign. Young W. A. was greatly taken with John Hicks, and one day he asked permission to leave school to attend the ten o'clock services at the church. Entering the chapel, he sat directly behind his mother and drank in every word that Hicks spoke. When Hicks gave the invitation, the lad went forward and, with tears, took Jesus Christ as his Savior.

Years later, when Criswell was a world-renowned

pastor, he recounted his conversion to a friend of his, Wallace Basset.

"Would you repeat that, W. A.?" Basset asked.

He repeated the story.

"I just can't imagine that," Basset said. "Johnny Hicks was a dear friend of mine, and he was here in Baylor Hospital in his last illness of which he died. I went often to see Johnny, and one day as I sat beside him, he said, 'Wallace, my life is over, my preaching days are done, and I've never done anything for Jesus. I've failed, Wallace, I've failed.' "

Those were the last words the old preacher ever spoke. He didn't realize how successful he had been in that one conversion.

J. O. Fraser, who worked for years among the Lisu of China before seeing multitudes come to Christ, once said, "I thoroughly agree with the assertion, 'all discouragement is from the devil.' Discouragement is to be resisted just like sin."

Those laboring for Christ are doing more good than we know, and only in heaven will we see the final scorecard.

"Therefore, my beloved brethren, be steadfast, immovable, always abounding in the work of the Lord, knowing that your labor is not in vain in the Lord" (1 Corinthians 15:58).

92

Shattered Glass

The most famous Chinese Christian of the twentieth century, Watchman Nee, once preached a sermon without saying a word. It was just as the Communists were swallowing up China, and Christians were coming under intense pressure to yield to the demands of the state. Churches were being closed and pastors slammed into jail. Because Watchman Nee was a widely-known and respected leader, many pastors and Christians looked to him for counsel. He was asked to address them at a meeting.

The great Christian faced a dilemma. If he spoke at this meeting, he was certain to be interrupted and arrested by government spies in the congregation before finishing his remarks. But if he didn't speak, he would disappoint those who most needed his courage and wisdom.

He came up with a solution that was very "Chinese," and very clever. He *mimed* his sermon. Standing in the pulpit, he looked out over the packed hall. The place fell to a hush. Picking up a glass of water, he stared at it with fierce countenance then hurled it to the floor, smashing it. Then he surveyed the broken pieces of glass with a smug, arrogant expression and spent the next five minutes walking around, crunching the glass under his feet.

Suddenly his expression changed to horror. Stooping down, he began sweeping up the shards of glass. He put the pieces on the pulpit and tried to reassemble them into a drinking glass, but it was impossible. Finally in despair he threw the pieces into the air. They scattered everywhere, and Watchman Nee walked away, his sermon finished.

The spies didn't know what to make of it, but the pastors understood completely, and they left the meeting greatly blessed.

Forty years later, a pastor in Shanghai explained the parable. He said, "Nee himself represented the state, and the glass represented the church. He was telling us that the state would try to smash the church, and for awhile it would look as if they had succeeded. But soon the state would realize it had made a terrible mistake, because in smashing the church it had not destroyed it, but dispersed it."

The parable proved prophetic. When missionaries were forced out of China in 1949, there were less than one million Christians, and the Communists were determined to wipe them out. But their attempts to destroy the church backfired, and instead of destroying it, they dispersed it. In the years since the Communist Revolution, China has experienced the largest and greatest revival in the history of the world. The last fifty years in China have been a reproduction of the book of Acts.*

*The chaos of persecution within China makes this story impossible to verify, and it may be apocryphal. It is included in an insightful paper by Alex Buchan, a Hong-Kong based reporter, titled, "The Chinese Revival—Coming to a Church Near You?" Watchman Nee was imprisoned for over twenty years by the Chinese Communists, dying June 1, 1972.

93

Never on Sunday

Jonathan Edwards fell in love with Sarah Pierrepont when she was thirteen. He was moody and stiff; she was as vivacious as a songbird. He could think of nothing but her, and one day studying Greek, he scribbled in the cover of his textbook that Sarah goes *from place to place, singing sweetly, full of joy. She loves to be alone, walking in the fields and groves, and seems to have someone invisible always conversing with her.*

They married on July 28, 1727, the bride (then seventeen) in a green dress. Jonathan was hired by a Massachusetts church. But parishioners often criticized the young couple. Jonathan was too strict for some, Sarah too extravagant for others.

Even worse, they evidently had sex on the Lord's Day. Colonial New Englanders believed that babies were born on the same day of the week as conceived. When six of the Edwards' eleven children arrived on Sundays, it sent tongues wagging. Such intimacy wasn't viewed as appropriate Sunday behavior.

But through all the hardships, the couple nurtured their love. They cherished afternoon horseback rides along forest trails during which they discussed everything from Jonathan's books to theology to child-rearing to world events. They had nightly devotions, and Jonathan read Sarah his compositions daily. He devoted an hour each day to the children and took them on trips one at a time.

George Whitefield wrote: *A sweeter couple I have not seen. Their children were not dressed in silks and satins, but plain, examples of Christian simplicity. Mrs. Edwards is adorned with a meek, quiet spirit; she talked solidly of the things of God, and seemed to be such a helpmeet for her husband, that she caused me to renew those prayers, I have put up to God, (for) a wife.*

Jonathan's last words were, *Give my love to my dear wife, and tell her that the uncommon union which has long subsisted between us has been of such a nature as I trust is spiritual and therefore will continue forever.*

Years later a reporter tracked down fourteen hundred descendants of Jonathan and Sarah, finding among them eighty college presidents, professors, and deans, one hundred lawyers, sixty-six physicians, eighty political leaders, three senators, three governors, countless preachers and missionaries—and one traitor, Aaron Burr. ❧

94

Sutter's Gold

Sometimes the sources of our happiness contain the seeds of our own destruction. Consider General John A. Sutter. On January 24, 1848, one of his workman, building a grist mill on the South fork of the American River, found a small yellow stone that appeared to be gold. The next morning at daybreak, the man rushed forty miles down the canyon to Sutter's ranch house with the exciting news. Sutter was elated, his heart filled with ultimate happiness. Gold on his land! Pure, yellow nuggets that would make him the richest man on earth.

Sutter tried to keep his discovery a secret, but within a day all his ranch hands had left their tasks in a mad frenzy, digging and panning and scratching for gold. Within a week, the whole countryside was in turmoil as ranches, towns, and villages were abandoned, everyone rushing to Sutter's ranch in search of gold.

Telegraph wires hummed, and soon soldiers were deserting from the army, fathers from their families, employees from their jobs, farmers from their ranches. By 1848 it seemed that half the country was camping on Sutter's ranch, digging for gold. Ships had no sooner docked in San Francisco Bay before the sailors jumped ship and headed for the hills.

John Sutter could only look on in helpless rage as his ranch was ransacked, his barns torn down, his crops trampled, and his cattle slaughtered. In time, he fought back by filing what was, at that time, the biggest lawsuit in history. He claimed that both San Francisco and Sacramento had been built on his property. He won the suit, but never received a penny. Mobs, enraged by the decision, burned the courthouse with its records and blew up Sutter's houses and barns with dynamite. They murdered one of his sons and drove another to commit suicide. A third son, attempting to flee the madness by going to Europe, drowned. John A. Sutter himself, staggering under these cruel blows, lost his reason.

For twenty years after that, he haunted the Capitol in Washington, trying to persuade Congress to recognize his rights. Dressed in rags, the poor, old, demented man went from one senator to another pleading for justice, and the children in the street laughed and jeered him as he passed.

In the spring of 1880, he died in a furnished room in Washington, alone and despised. He didn't have a dollar when he passed away, though he did possess a legal deed to the greatest fortune on earth.*

If only we better comprehended our Lord's words: "Take heed and beware of covetousness, for one's life does not consist in the abundance of the things he possesses" (Luke 12:15).

*Adapted from Dale Carnegie, *Little Known Facts About Well Known People* (New York: Blue Ribbon Books, Inc., 1934), pp. 6–10.

95

I Need This Sugar

Russell and Darlene Deibler were welcomed as missionaries to New Guinea in 1938 by an old and distinguished British missionary, Dr. Robert Alexander Jaffray. When, during World War II, the Japanese invaded the island, Dr. Jaffray was with them. The Japanese seized Russell and the other male missionaries, hauling them to concentration camps. Darlene never saw her husband again. But Dr. Jaffray, being aged and ill, was allowed to remain with the women, which included Margaret Jaffray, his daughter.

Margaret was extremely careful about the foods she prepared for her father, because of Dr. Jaffray's diabetic condition. She and Darlene had stockpiled as much saccharin as they could, for use in recipes calling for sugar. But the supplies were very limited, for the war had cut them off from all external provisions.

One afternoon after a tiring walk, Dr. Jaffray, Margaret, and Darlene collapsed into chairs for tea. Margaret prepared tea and set the tray on a small table near her father. He helped himself to milk, and, instead of taking saccharin, he picked up the sugar bowl and spooned one, two, three teaspoons of sugar into his tea. The women couldn't believe their eyes, and Margaret was horrified. "Daddy," she pleaded, "please don't do that. You know you aren't supposed to have sugar."

Remembering that he had recently been in a diabetic coma and understanding her fears, he tried to reassure her. "Muggie," he said, "I'm healed. I need this sugar for strength." He continued to use sugar, and when she begged that he not use so much, he patted her hand, saying, "It's all right, Muggie. I'm healed."

Not too many days later, the women were able to smuggle a urine specimen to a local Dutch doctor with a message: "For several days now Dr. Jaffray has been using sugar. He believes the Lord has healed him, but we would like confirmation."

A few days later a letter was smuggled back. The doctor had examine the specimen and found not a trace of sugar. Dr. Jaffray had indeed been healed.

Darlene later wrote, "We had a time of praising and

thanking the Lord. He was preparing Dr. Jaffray for a time when there would be no saccharin, only scant rations of sugar. The Lord is very good to those who put their trust in Him." ❧

96

Now It Was My Turn

Curtis Bradford, a pastor in Charleston, South Carolina, said that when he was seven years old he crawled into bed on Christmas Eve so excited he couldn't sleep. Pretending to be asleep, he lay there until he was sure his parents were snoring. Then, about 2 A.M., he crept downstairs.

There under the Christmas trees were his presents. A drum set beckoned him to play it then and there, but he didn't dare. But he found other gifts he could play with. A cowboy outfit, a set of six-shooters, a puppet. Filled with excitement, he emptied his stocking, began eating the candy, the apple, the orange. . . . But suddenly, hearing a noise, he turned and say his dad looking sternly down at him.

For a fleeting moment, Curtis was afraid, but his dad broke into a smile, settled himself in the recliner, and listened while Curtis showed him everything, explaining how the six-shooters worked and how the puppet moved its mouth.

Sleep soon came over him, and his dad picked him up, carried him upstairs, and tenderly tucked him into bed. The next morning they had a wonderful Christmas, but, Curtis said, "I will never forget that Christmas Eve."

The years flew by, and, on another memorable Christmas, Curtis found himself again at his father's side. This time the older man lay paralyzed from an automobile accident and weak from cancer. Treatments, therapy, and experimental drugs had left him weighing less than one hundred pounds and in great pain. But despite his pain, he asked if Curtis would dress him so he could watch the family open presents. He wanted a cleanly shaven face. So Curtis lathered the shaving mug and brush and got out the razor to shave his dad. The old man told him how his beard grew this way and that, and how he needed to turn the razor up at one point and down at another.

After the shave, Curtis dressed him and carried him to the den where the family waited. He was able to sit there for almost fifteen minutes before the joy turned to almost unbearable pain. Then his eyes filled with tears, and he asked Curtis to carry him back to bed. Gently, the strong adult son gathered the frail man into his arms. Curtis later said, "As I made my way to his bedroom, I recalled the night many years before when he had carried me to my bedroom after our private Christmas showing. Now it was my turn to carry him."

Tears ran down Curtis' face as he nestled his dad into bed, and seeing the tears, the old man pointed to a tape recorder beside the bed. Curtis turned it on, and together they listened to the Bible being read. It was John 14: "In My Father's house there are many mansions. . . ." Silently Curtis thanked God for saving him, for saving his father, for giving them those moments together, and for those times when the Lord had carried them both.

Two days later, Curtis' dad passed away. But the memories are precious rather than painful, says Curtis. "Because of Jesus, whose birth we celebrate on Christmas and who died to save those who believe in Him, I know I will see may father again. And what a family reunion that will be."*

*Adapted from the article "Gifts From My Father" by Curtis Bradford in *Experiencing God* Magazine, December 1995, 16–17.

97

That Half-Crazy Cruden

One of my first Bible study books was *Cruden's Concordance,* a famous old work that lists many of the words that occur in the Bible and gives their references. My father used his *Cruden's Concordance* faithfully, and at an early age I began doing the same. Christians of many generations have located verses of Scripture by pulling their *Cruden's Concordance* off its shelf. Spurgeon wrote in the flyleaf of his, "For ten years this has been at my left hand when the Word of God has been at my right."

Here's the rest of the story: Alexander Cruden was born in Scotland on May 31, 1699. His father, a strict Puritan, forbade games on the Lord's Day, and Alexander entertained himself by tracing words through the Bible. He enrolled in college at age thirteen, graduated at age nineteen, and fell in love. The girl's father forbade him to be in their house, and when the girl became pregnant, she was sent away. Alexander, his nerves broken, entered an asylum.

In 1726, he was hired to read books aloud for Lord Derby of Sussex. Alexander began reading the way he always did—spelling out each word letter by letter. He was quickly fired, but he refused to leave the grounds. For months, he followed Lord Derby around, creating one scene after another. He eventually moved to London and began working on his *Concordance*. It was published in 1737 and became an immediate success.

Alexander fell in love again, was rejected again, and went to such extremes to attract the woman's affection that he was seized, taken to a private asylum, and chained to a bed for ten weeks. He finally managed to escape by cutting off the bed leg, then began traveling around calling himself "Alexander the Corrector," trying to reform morals. One evening, wanting to stop a man from swearing, he hit him over the head with a shovel. A riot ensued, and Alexander endured a third stay in an asylum. Being released, he fell in love again, was rejected again, and badgered the king to appoint him "Alexander the Corrector."

People thought him crazy—but they loved his *Con-*

cordance. Alexander spent his final days giving out tracts and studying the Bible. One morning in 1770, a servant found him on his knees, his head on the open Bible, dead. "This half crazy Cruden," said Spurgeon, "did better service to the church than half the D.D.'s and L.L.D.'s of all time."

98

Afraid? Of That?

The years leading up to World War II were very dangerous for missionaries to China. Political uproar, bandits, the Japanese Invasion, and the Communist Revolution caused many of them to fear for their lives.

One of the missionaries, Jack Vinson, was seized by bandits and carried off in the night. He was eventually shot and beheaded. A witness later described how earlier she had seen Vinson threatened by a bandit with a revolver who said, "I'm going to kill you! Aren't you afraid?"

"No, I am not afraid," Vinson had replied. "If you kill me, I will go right to God."

The news of Vinson's martyrdom deeply moved the Christians in China. When missionary E. H. Hamilton heard the story after emerging from another bandit-infested area, he wrote a poem that became the watchword for the missionary community during the dark days that followed. It was this poem that strengthened John and Betty Stam, among others, before their martyrdom.

It said simply:

Afraid? Of What?
To feel the spirit's glad release?
To pass from pain to perfect peace,
The strife and strain of life to cease?
Afraid—of that?

Afraid? Of What?
Afraid to see the Savior's face
To hear his welcome, and to trace
The glory gleam from wounds of grace?
Afraid—of that?

Afraid? Of What?
A flash, a crash, a pierced heart;
Darkness, light, O Heaven's art!
A wound of His a counterpart?
Afraid—of that?

Afraid? Of What?
To do by death what life could not—
Baptized with blood a stony plot,
Till souls shall blossom from the spot?
Afraid—of that?

99

Deceived

In his book *Bones of Contention,* professor Marvin Lubenow tells the sad story of Sir Arthur Keith, one of the greatest anatomists of the twentieth century. According to Keith's autobiography, as a young man he attended evangelistic meetings in Edinburgh and Aberdeen and watched students make their commitments to Jesus Christ. He himself often felt on "the verge of conversion," yet he resisted, rejecting the gospel because he felt that the Genesis account of creation was just a myth and that the Bible was merely a human book.

Later, as a scientist, Keith became greatly intrigued by a famous discovery in England. In 1908, forty miles from downtown London, in a gravel pit near the village of Piltdown, some bones were "discovered," portions of a human skull, a molar, and a lower jaw. Soon it was announced to the Geological Society of London that these were the remains of the earliest known Englishman, *Eoanthropus dawsoni,* otherwise known as Piltdown Man. The vast majority of paleontologists worldwide hailed this as a great discovery of our potential human ancestors.

The literature produced on Piltdown man was enormous. It is said that more than five hundred doctoral dissertations were written about him. To Sir Arthur Keith, it was the validation of his evolutionary beliefs—the missing link—and he wrote more on Piltdown Man than anyone else. His famous work, *The Antiquity of Man,* centered on Piltdown. Much of his life was spent studying and proclaiming the wonders of this discovery.

Though the Piltdown fossils were discovered between 1908 and 1915, it was not until 1953 that the British Museum proclaimed the entire thing was a fraud. The jawbone was not much older than the year it was found. The bones had been treated with iron salts to make them appear old, and scratch marks were detected in the teeth, indicating that they had been filed.

Sir Arthur Keith was eighty-six years old when his colleagues visited him at his home to break the news that the fossil he had trusted in for forty years was a hoax.

A great scholar had rejected the witness of both God's natural creation and the Lord Jesus, whose resurrection validated everything He said and did, only to put a lifetime of misplaced faith in what proved to be a phony fossil. ❧

100

Criticism

When Fiorello La Guardia was the mayor of New York City (1933–1945), he hung above his desk in City Hall, a pronouncement by Abraham Lincoln.

Interestingly, General MacArthur had a copy of it hanging over his headquarters desk during World War II, and Winston Churchill had a framed copy of it on the walls of his study at Chartwell.

It said:

If I were to try to read, much less answer, all the attacks made on me, this shop might as well be closed for any other business. I do the very best I know how—the very best I can, and I mean to keep doing so until the end. If the end brings me out all right, what is said against me won't amount to anything. If the end brings me out wrong, ten angels swearing I was right would make no difference.

As I've faced occasional criticism over one thing or another, I've often thought of an Oriental proverb I once read: *The dogs bark, but the caravan passes.*

Charles Spurgeon once said, "Fault-finding is dreadfully catching; one dog will set a whole kennel howling."

Our best response to criticism is to ask God if the complaint is valid. If it is, we need to change. If it isn't, just ignore it. Remember Augustine's prayer: *O Lord, deliver me from this lust of always vindicating myself.*

101

Only One Message

Billy Graham once recalled, "I remember preaching in Dallas, Texas, early in our ministry. It was 1953. About forty-thousand people attended each night, but one evening only a few people responded to the appeal to receive Jesus Christ. Discouraged, I left the platform. A German businessman was there, a devout man of God. He put his arm around me and said, 'Billy, do you know what was wrong tonight? You didn't preach the cross.'

"The next night I preached on the blood of Christ, and a great host of people responded to receive Christ as Savior. When we proclaim the gospel of Christ, when we preach Christ crucified and risen, there is a built-in power to it."

One hundred years before, a reporter attending the great British evangelistic campaigns of evangelist D. L.

Moody wrote something remarkably similar. Referring to the great crowds attending Moody's meetings, the London journalist wrote, "One cannot but ask the question, 'What is the magic power which draws together these mighty multitudes and holds them spellbound?' Is it the worldly rank or wealth of learning or oratory of the preacher? No, for he is possessed of little of these. It is the simple lifting up of the cross of Christ—the holding forth the Lord Jesus before the eyes of the people."

Several years ago, we entertained a delightful woman in our home, Rosemaria Von Trapp, one of the famous "Sound of Music" children. I asked her about her parents, Captain Georg and Maria Von Trapp, who fled Nazi-occupied Austria because they refused to cooperate with the Nazis. She replied, "Only yesterday I talked to high-school students—sophomores—who were doing research papers on the Holocaust of Hitler in Germany. They wanted me to talk about the Nazis. I told them that Hitler gave us a symbol of a cross with hooks on it. But our Christian faith gives us a symbol of a cross that brings freedom and resurrection. The world, you know, offers us a glossy cross with hooks in it. My father and mother had to make a choice. They chose the cross of Christ."

No wonder the apostle Paul said, "The message of the cross is foolishness to those who are perishing, but to us who are being saved it is the power of God" (1 Corinthians 1:18). Let us cling to the old rugged cross, and exchange it some day for a crown. ❧

INDICES

Topical Index

Aging 34–35; 171–172
Atheism 63–65
Baptism 109–110
Child Evangelism 254–256
Christmas 157–160; 257–258; 276–278
Conversion Stories 15–16; 43–44; 69–70; 77–81; 87–88; 101–102; 117–118; 154–156; 227–229; 243–245
Creationism 63–65; 285–287
Criticism 288–289
Cross of Christ 290–292
Depression; Discouragement 4–6; 47–48; 103–107; 186–188; 238–239; 259–263
Dreams 17–19; 84–86; 249–250
Emptiness 131–134
Encouragement 8; 177
Failure 103–107; 60–62; 122–123; 203–204; 233–235
Forgiveness 10–11; 211–214; 236–237
Friendship 135–136
Gambling 243–245
Giving/Tithing 251–253

Healing 273–275
Hell 221–222
Humility and Pride 108; 178–180
Hymn Stories 4–6; 40–42; 137–140; 171–172; 186–188; 215–218; 238–239
Loneliness 7
Marriage 87–88; 119–121; 184–185; 267–269
Missions 12–14; 20–22; 36–37; 45–46; 59–52; 54–56; 60–62; 66–68; 71–73; 115–116; 124–125; 273–275
Persecution 31–33; 38–39, 54–56; 66–68; 74–76; 230–232; 240–242; 264–266; 282–284
Prayer 1–3; 4–6; 12–14; 27–30, 49–52; 53; 173–176; 189–192
Prayer Before Meals 27–30; 93
Revival 137–140; 224–226
Singing 144–146; 198–202
Small Churches 103–107
Smoking 117–118; 147–149
Sunday worship 57–59; 267–269
Titanic 189–192
Tears 161–165
Temptation 129–130; 147–149
Thanksgiving 181–183
Walking 99–100
Witnessing 99–100; 115–116; 173–176
Worry 111–114; 238–239

Scripture Index

Numbers 6:22–27 193–197
Deuteronomy 33:27 208–210
2 Kings 2:14 94–98
Psalm 19:1 63–65
Psalm 27:10 47–48
Psalm 31:15 84–86
Psalm 37 111–114
Psalm 50:15 49–52
Psalm 55:22 4–6
Psalm 84:10 119–121
Psalm 85:6 224–226
Psalm 103:12 10–11
Psalm 107 124–125
Psalm 119:11 198–202
Proverbs 15:1 246–248
Proverbs 24:16 233–235
Ecclesiastes 9:10 166–170
Isaiah 1:18 257–258
Isaiah 53:5 47–48
Isaiah 54:4 7
Jeremiah 31:16–17 71–73
Micah 2:10 89–91
Matthew 3:7 215–218
Matthew 5:44 227–229
Luke 12:15 270–272
Luke 15 101–102
John 4:35 20–22
John 6:37 40–42
John 9:25 36–37
John 10:10 131–134
John 14:1–6 276–278
John 15 103–107; 171–172
John 15:15 45–46
Acts 9:4 117–118
Romans 12:1–2 141–143
Romans 12:18 246–248
Romans 13:14 129–130
1 Corinthians 1:18 290–292

1 Corinthians 10:13	147–149	Ephesians 5:18–19	144–146
1 Corinthians 15:9–11	211–214	Philippians 2:14–16	246–248
1 Corinthians 15:58	259–263	Colossians 3:23	166–170
2 Corinthians 2:14	150–153	2 Timothy 3:15	254–256
2 Corinthians 5:17	154–156	James 5:16	27–30
Ephesians 4:24	166–170	1 Peter 5:7	4–6

If you have an interesting story, we would like to see it! Please e-mail it to pastor@donelson.org, and it may be included in a future edition of *Real Stories for the Soul.* Stories should be between 50 and 600 words and contain fact, not fiction. By submitting it, we will assume your permission to edit and use it should we choose. While we're unable to respond to each submission and cannot guarantee its inclusion in an upcoming book, please be assured we will read and consider every story.

Check your local Christian bookstore for other titles by Robert J. Morgan!

Real Stories for the Soul

101 stories to challenge your faith and strengthen your trust in God.
ISBN: 1-7852-4516-2

Nelson's Complete Book of Stories, Illustrations, & Quotes

The ultimate goldmine for speakers—humorous, serious, thought-provoking, and heart-warming material. Thousands of real-life stories, illustrations, and quotes indexed by subject and Scripture.
ISBN: 0-7852-4479-4

On This Day

365 amazing and inspiring stories about saints, martyrs, and heroes focusing on the hope God's Word can give when we need it most.
ISBN: 0-7852-1162-4

From This Verse

365 inspiring stories about the power of God's Word provide a wealth of ideas and colorful illustrations for sermons and Bible lessons, as well as being ideal for devotional use.
ISBN: 0-7852-1393-7